JUMBLE®
Geography

Where in the World Are the Best Puzzles?!

Henri Arnold,
Bob Lee,
Mike Argirion,
Jeff Knurek, &
David L. Hoyt

TRIUMPH
BOOKS

This book is available in quantity at special discounts
for your group or organization.

For further information, contact:

Triumph Books LLC
814 North Franklin Street
Chicago, Illinois 60610
Phone: (312) 337-0747
www.triumphbooks.com

Printed in U.S.A.

ISBN: 978-1-62937-615-8

Design by Sue Knopf

Contents

JUMBLE® Geography

Classic Puzzles

JUMBLE.

Unscramble these four Jumbles, one letter
to each square, to form four ordinary words.

MATID

GAUVE

BLEANE

SHUBLE

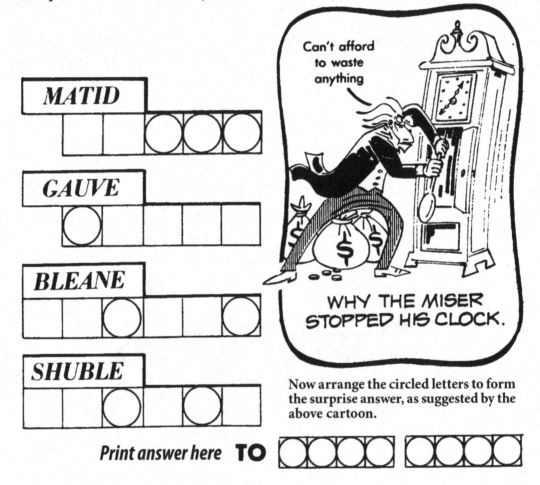

Can't afford
to waste
anything

WHY THE MISER
STOPPED HIS CLOCK.

Now arrange the circled letters to form
the surprise answer, as suggested by the
above cartoon.

Print answer here TO

JUMBLE®

Unscramble these four Jumbles, one letter to each square, to form four ordinary words.

TIFUR

NERTY

EXDULE

DIMFOY

WHAT SHE SAID WHEN SHE SAW A MINK.

Now arrange the circled letters to form the surprise answer, as suggested by the above cartoon.

Print answer here

" I KNOW WHAT ⬡⬡⬡ ' ⬡⬡ ⬡⬡⬡ "

JUMBLE®

Unscramble these four Jumbles, one letter
to each square, to form four ordinary words.

EAZUG

MELIP

REPACT

NETOED

THIS COULD BE *ELEGANT.*

Now arrange the circled letters to form
the surprise answer, as suggested by the
above cartoon.

Print answer here ⬡⬡⬡⬡ ⬡⬡⬡

JUMBLE®

Unscramble these four Jumbles, one letter
to each square, to form four ordinary words.

ALLIV

NORTS

THEIRE

UNCOBE

SOMETHING NEW
IN NECKWEAR.

Now arrange the circled letters to form
the surprise answer, as suggested by the
above cartoon.

Print answer here " ☐◯◯◯◯◯ – ☐◯◯◯☐ "

JUMBLE®

Unscramble these four Jumbles, one letter
to each square, to form four ordinary words.

MORGO

CHITH

GIRFID

FRAITY

SHE DOESN'T LIKE
TO RECEIVE ONE
OR LOOK ONE.

Now arrange the circled letters to form
the surprise answer, as suggested by the
above cartoon.

Print answer here **A** ◯◯◯◯◯◯◯

JUMBLE®

Unscramble these four Jumbles, one letter to each square, to form four ordinary words.

MAGEL

ORNOH

LIDBOY

WAIRND

Low pay . . . don't have much to put in . . .

EH?

MIGHT BE A SOUND INVESTMENT FOR THOSE WHO DON'T GET EVERYTHING.

Now arrange the circled letters to form the surprise answer, as suggested by the above cartoon.

Print answer here **A** ⬡◯◯◯◯◯◯◯ ◯◯◯

JUMBLE®

Unscramble these four Jumbles, one letter
to each square, to form four ordinary words.

DARNB

ZEFOR

LOCASE

YARWIA

VOLUNTEERS

LET'S BEAT HIM!

ONE **USED** TO BE THIS IN OR AT WHEN HE ENLISTED.

Now arrange the circled letters to form
the surprise answer, as suggested by the
above cartoon.

Print answer here

JUMBLE®

Unscramble these four Jumbles, one letter to each square, to form four ordinary words.

TREHB

PINYP

INMALY

CLUMON

MEN IN PORT ARE CONSPICUOUS.

Now arrange the circled letters to form the surprise answer, as suggested by the above cartoon.

Print answer here " "

PUZZLE 9

JUMBLE®

Unscramble these four Jumbles, one letter to each square, to form four ordinary words.

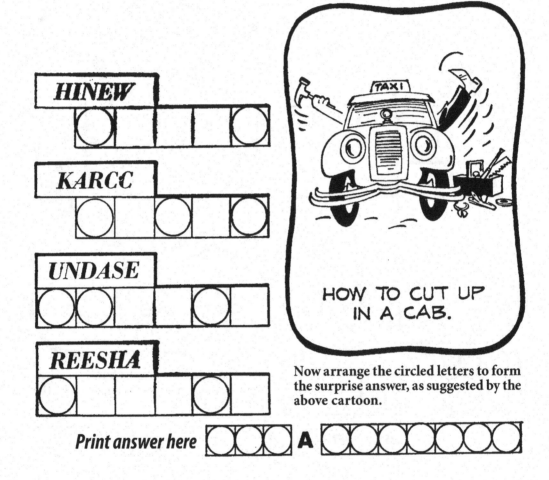

HINEW

KARCC

UNDASE

REESHA

HOW TO CUT UP IN A CAB.

Now arrange the circled letters to form the surprise answer, as suggested by the above cartoon.

Print answer here ◯◯◯ A ◯◯◯◯◯◯◯

JUMBLE®

Unscramble these four Jumbles, one letter
to each square, to form four ordinary words.

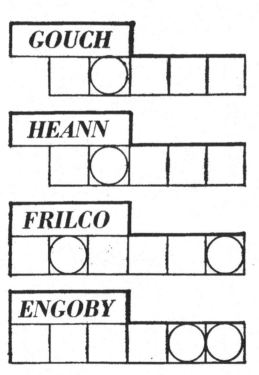

GOUCH

HEANN

FRILCO

ENGOBY

Again in France?

Now arrange the circled letters to form
the surprise answer, as suggested by the
above cartoon.

Print answer here  " "

JUMBLE®

Unscramble these four Jumbles, one letter
to each square, to form four ordinary words.

ECHLE

MOBOL

GLENET

AMMBLE

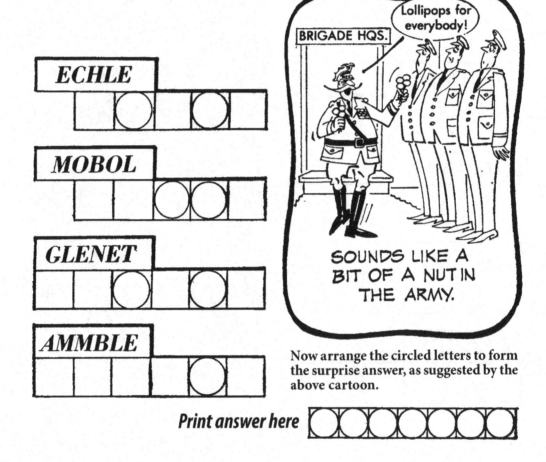

BRIGADE HQS.

Lollipops for everybody!

SOUNDS LIKE A
BIT OF A NUT IN
THE ARMY.

Now arrange the circled letters to form
the surprise answer, as suggested by the
above cartoon.

Print answer here

JUMBLE®

Unscramble these four Jumbles, one letter
to each square, to form four ordinary words.

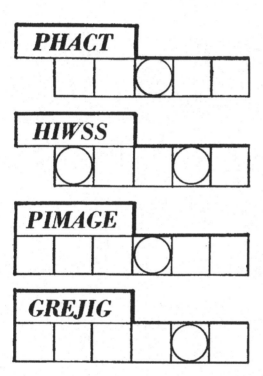

PHACT

HIWSS

PIMAGE

GREJIG

SEVERAL IN
A FLIGHT.

Now arrange the circled letters to form
the surprise answer, as suggested by the
above cartoon.

Print answer here

JUMBLE®

Unscramble these four Jumbles, one letter
to each square, to form four ordinary words.

OOCCA

THYAS

PRONED

KLEACT

Have you heard
the latest . . . ?

Drink up and
shut up!

THIS DRINK MIGHT
PUT AN END
TO RUMORS.

Now arrange the circled letters to form
the surprise answer, as suggested by the
above cartoon.

Print answer here

JUMBLE®

Unscramble these four Jumbles, one letter to each square, to form four ordinary words.

RAYIF

LOCON

UNNOIB

TREEMP

Now arrange the circled letters to form the surprise answer, as suggested by the above cartoon.

Print answer here " ⬡⬡⬡⬡⬡⬡⬡ "

JUMBLE®

Unscramble these four Jumbles, one letter
to each square, to form four ordinary words.

CADUL

TIFFY

MACENE

DIONIE

NOT TO BE PLAYED
WITH WHEN LOADED.

Now arrange the circled letters to form
the surprise answer, as suggested by the
above cartoon.

Print answer here ◯◯◯◯

JUMBLE®

Unscramble these four Jumbles, one letter to each square, to form four ordinary words.

KLEAY

SIPOE

THALEC

CHYPIS

Don't try to fool me

FAR FROM ALERT BUT OUTWARDLY SLY.

Now arrange the circled letters to form the surprise answer, as suggested by the above cartoon.

Print answer here " ⬡⬡ – ⬡⬡⬡ – ⬡ "

JUMBLE®

Unscramble these four Jumbles, one letter
to each square, to form four ordinary words.

PREKO

CAIBS

LURCUN

SPOCER

A KIND OF EUROPEAN
CURTAIN MATERIAL.

Now arrange the circled letters to form
the surprise answer, as suggested by the
above cartoon.

Print answer here 〇〇〇〇

JUMBLE®

Unscramble these four Jumbles, one letter
to each square, to form four ordinary words.

NOKTE

SKUYH

TIBBEG

GOFTER

WHEN DROPPED ARE
MEANT TO BE TAKEN
UP BY SOMEONE ELSE.

Now arrange the circled letters to form
the surprise answer, as suggested by the
above cartoon.

Print answer here

JUMBLE.

Unscramble these four Jumbles, one letter
to each square, to form four ordinary words.

GEWED

CITOX

LEMPOC

PANOWE

DRAGGED AWAY—TO
GET MARRIED.

Now arrange the circled letters to form
the surprise answer, as suggested by the
above cartoon.

Print answer here "◯◯ - ◯◯◯"

JUMBLE®

Unscramble these four Jumbles, one letter
to each square, to form four ordinary words.

NIORB

PUTIL

WODASH

YOGAVE

So nice of you to come

YOU WOULDN'T EXPECT
TO FIND HER
AT HOME!

Now arrange the circled letters to form
the surprise answer, as suggested by the
above cartoon.

Print answer here **A** ☐☐☐☐☐☐☐☐

21

JUMBLE®

Unscramble these four Jumbles, one letter to each square, to form four ordinary words.

DENEY

SURUP

REGEME

KOVINE

WHERE AN ASTRONOMER MIGHT FIND POETRY.

Now arrange the circled letters to form the surprise answer, as suggested by the above cartoon.

Print answer here **IN THE** "◯◯◯-◯◯◯◯◯"

JUMBLE®

Unscramble these four Jumbles, one letter
to each square, to form four ordinary words.

ADGEL

GLEEY

DIMRAY

TURBAP

WHAT YOU'LL FIND IN
THE ROOM OF
YOUR DREAMS.

Now arrange the circled letters to form
the surprise answer, as suggested by the
above cartoon.

Print answer here

JUMBLE®

Unscramble these four Jumbles, one letter
to each square, to form four ordinary words.

DESTE

YAILG

BASHUM

CYMALL

Cover up!

ZOO

NO SUN-BATHING

MIGHT BE BARRED
IN SOME PARKS.

Now arrange the circled letters to form
the surprise answer, as suggested by the
above cartoon.

Print answer here

JUMBLE®

Unscramble these four Jumbles, one letter
to each square, to form four ordinary words.

BUGOH

TELUF

KEENAW

DANGIR

Tsk! Tsk!
Dead
battery!

YOU MIGHT BE
POWERLESS
TO ACCEPT THIS.

Now arrange the circled letters to form
the surprise answer, as suggested by the
above cartoon.

Print answer here

JUMBLE®

Unscramble these four Jumbles, one letter to each square, to form four ordinary words.

TEYIP

DITAU

MERMAH

TAMLED

Time to wash up for dinner!

IT'S ALWAYS DONE IN THE EVENING!

Now arrange the circled letters to form the surprise answer, as suggested by the above cartoon.

Print answer here ◯◯◯ ◯◯◯

JUMBLE® Geography

JUMBLE®

Unscramble these four Jumbles, one letter
to each square, to form four ordinary words.

ELVOG

UPTYT

WILDEM

GRUBEO

HOW TO SELL AN
ELECTRICAL GADGET.

Now arrange the circled letters to form
the surprise answer, as suggested by the
above cartoon.

Print answer here

JUMBLE®

Unscramble these four Jumbles, one letter
to each square, to form four ordinary words.

INYAR

HALET

CALVEE

FLAUDE

I want 'em spotless!

WORKING HE GETS
ALL *THE DIRTIER.*

Now arrange the circled letters to form
the surprise answer, as suggested by the
above cartoon.

Print answer here

JUMBLE®

Unscramble these four Jumbles, one letter
to each square, to form four ordinary words.

CANTE

YADEC

CABEEM

RATTEP

RESTAURANT

LIVERY
ANCE

TAKEN DOWN INSIDE.

Now arrange the circled letters to form
the surprise answer, as suggested by the
above cartoon.

Print answer here ⟨◯◯◯◯◯⟩

JUMBLE®

Unscramble these four Jumbles, one letter
to each square, to form four ordinary words.

PHRAC

SNUKK

FLACIE

YARNEL

Nice guy—just moved in

WHAT THAT PORTUGUESE
NEIGHBOR IS.

Now arrange the circled letters to form
the surprise answer, as suggested by the
above cartoon.

Print answer here 〇〇〇〇〇

JUMBLE®

Unscramble these four Jumbles, one letter to each square, to form four ordinary words.

SIBAN

CAXTE

DESAUB

ANCIDD

Tomorrow's assignment takes us down to other worlds

LITERATURE 101

MADE A DENT IN THE HISTORY OF LITERATURE.

Now arrange the circled letters to form the surprise answer, as suggested by the above cartoon.

Print answer here ⃝⃝⃝⃝⃝

JUMBLE®

Unscramble these four Jumbles, one letter to each square, to form four ordinary words.

NAGIT

LYDIO

DILBOE

TYKONT

I felt a kick

WHAT THE BILLY GOAT
SAID TO HIS MATE.

Now arrange the circled letters to form the surprise answer, as suggested by the above cartoon.

Print answer here **YOU'RE** ⬡⬡⬡⬡⬡⬡⬡!

JUMBLE®

Unscramble these four Jumbles, one letter
to each square, to form four ordinary words.

TENFO

ITUSE

RUGLAF

YORTHE

It HAD been
so peaceful!

A LOUD CRY THAT'S
QUIET TO START WITH.

Now arrange the circled letters to form
the surprise answer, as suggested by the
above cartoon.

Print answer here " ☐☐ - ☐☐☐ "

34

JUMBLE®

Unscramble these four Jumbles, one letter
to each square, to form four ordinary words.

WOPOH

UNEES

TADEEB

ENMURB

Who's the big boss here?

It's a raid!

HOW THEY KNEW HE
WAS THE PROPRIETOR.

Now arrange the circled letters to form
the surprise answer, as suggested by the
above cartoon.

Print answer here HE

JUMBLE®

Unscramble these four Jumbles, one letter
to each square, to form four ordinary words.

CHURS

TOIDT

BLENGO

KLINTE

Let's play
with the
new train

WHAT YOU MIGHT
FEEL LIKE DOING
AFTER DINNER.

Now arrange the circled letters to form
the surprise answer, as suggested by the
above cartoon.

Print answer here

JUMBLE®

Unscramble these four Jumbles, one letter
to each square, to form four ordinary words.

SEBEO

CEIPE

TERLIP

NAFELL

AN EDIBLE PART
OF POPPIES THAT
MANY BECOME
ADDICTED TO.

Now arrange the circled letters to form
the surprise answer, as suggested by the
above cartoon.

Print answer here "◯◯◯◯"

JUMBLE.®

Unscramble these four Jumbles, one letter
to each square, to form four ordinary words.

LAGEE

METHY

DOEKOH

SYTHAN

Snob!

WHAT "A MAN
OF LEISURE" MIGHT
LOOK DOWN AT.

Now arrange the circled letters to form
the surprise answer, as suggested by the
above cartoon.

Print answer here ☐◯◯◯☐ ☐◯◯◯◯◯☐

JUMBLE®

Unscramble these four Jumbles, one letter
to each square, to form four ordinary words.

SASIB

TREXE

GRECLY

CALHUN

Going to the paddock—
back in a minute

SHOW

PLACE

CHECKS ON A HORSE!

Now arrange the circled letters to form
the surprise answer, as suggested by the
above cartoon.

Print answer here

JUMBLE®

Unscramble these four Jumbles, one letter
to each square, to form four ordinary words.

STRYT

ESING

LUBOSE

RETAUM

Won't you come to my studio?

ONE WHO WON'T STAND FOR BEING PAINTED.

Now arrange the circled letters to form
the surprise answer, as suggested by the
above cartoon.

Print answer here **A**

JUMBLE®

Unscramble these four Jumbles, one letter
to each square, to form four ordinary words.

NOICT

SNOBI

KOYDEN

LEWLOY

LOOT TAKEN FROM
A SHOE STORE.

Now arrange the circled letters to form
the surprise answer, as suggested by the
above cartoon.

Print answer here " ◯◯◯◯ – ◯ "

JUMBLE®

Unscramble these four Jumbles, one letter
to each square, to form four ordinary words.

ELZAH

LORGY

INOUSC

DRIAFA

He wants to attack

But how'll he buy the guns?

WHAT THE GENERAL
SAID WHEN THEY
RAN OUT OF MONEY
TO FIGHT THE WAR.

Now arrange the circled letters to form
the surprise answer, as suggested by the
above cartoon.

Print answer here

JUMBLE®

Unscramble these four Jumbles, one letter to each square, to form four ordinary words.

LAURR

MAIDT

NESING

THUBOG

Guess what it says about you for today!

WHAT HE SAID
ALL THAT ASTROLOGY
BULL WAS.

Now arrange the circled letters to form the surprise answer, as suggested by the above cartoon.

Print answer here "◯◯◯◯◯◯"

JUMBLE®

Unscramble these four Jumbles, one letter
to each square, to form four ordinary words.

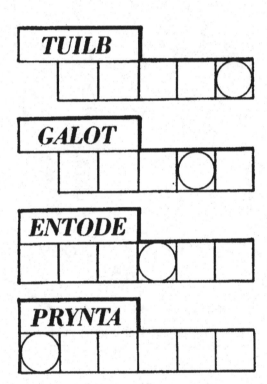

TUILB

GALOT

ENTODE

PRYNTA

What's it
gonna be?

WHAT THE
CERAMICS WORKER
WAS DEVELOPING.

Now arrange the circled letters to form
the surprise answer, as suggested by the
above cartoon.

Print answer here

JUMBLE®

Unscramble these four Jumbles, one letter
to each square, to form four ordinary words.

ROODE

MOBZI

RENOSP

HAWRTT

A TRAVELER HAS
ABSOLUTELY NO
CHANCE OF GETTING
ON THIS LINE!

Now arrange the circled letters to form
the surprise answer, as suggested by the
above cartoon.

Print answer here **THE** ◯◯◯◯◯◯◯◯

JUMBLE®

Unscramble these four Jumbles, one letter
to each square, to form four ordinary words.

PEXLE

LUFAW

MISTEY

TASTLE

THE RUNNER
SATISFIED HIS
THIRST AFTER THIS.

Now arrange the circled letters to form
the surprise answer, as suggested by the
above cartoon.

Print answer here **A** ⬚⬚⬚⬚ ⬚⬚⬚⬚⬚

JUMBLE®

Unscramble these four Jumbles, one letter
to each square, to form four ordinary words.

LEERD

IMPER

TIGBLE

BLOGIE

Breakfast
is ready

Hope she
doesn't burn
the bacon
again

YOU WOULDN'T EAT IT
WHEN IN THIS!

Now arrange the circled letters to form
the surprise answer, as suggested by the
above cartoon.

Print answer here " – – ◯◯◯◯◯◯ "

JUMBLE®

Unscramble these four Jumbles, one letter
to each square, to form four ordinary words.

MEZIA

THRAW

ROWDYS

GONEPS

Not
tonight,
dear

WHY SHE ALWAYS HAD
SOMETHING ON WHEN-
EVER HE ASKED FOR
A DATE.

Now arrange the circled letters to form
the surprise answer, as suggested by the
above cartoon.

Print answer here **SHE** ⬡⬡⬡ ⬡⬡⬡⬡⬡⬡

JUMBLE®

Unscramble these four Jumbles, one letter
to each square, to form four ordinary words.

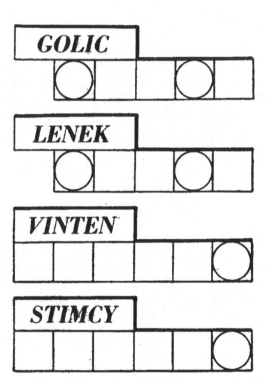

GOLIC

LENEK

VINTEN

STIMCY

THIS LIGHT TOUCH
COULD PRODUCE
LAUGHTER IN THE
THEATER.

Now arrange the circled letters to form
the surprise answer, as suggested by the
above cartoon.

Print answer here **A**

JUMBLE®

Unscramble these four Jumbles, one letter to each square, to form four ordinary words.

RAPPE

BECAL

ZEFRYN

HORDIA

I'm going to bake a cake

FOLLOWED IN THE KITCHEN.

Now arrange the circled letters to form the surprise answer, as suggested by the above cartoon.

Print answer here A

JUMBLE®

Unscramble these four Jumbles, one letter to each square, to form four ordinary words.

YASAS

KORJE

RATOOR

TANQUI

PRIVATE

Guess I'm the only one who does anything here!

THE REMAINDER DOESN'T WORK.

Now arrange the circled letters to form the surprise answer, as suggested by the above cartoon.

Print answer here " ◯◯◯◯ "

JUMBLE®

Unscramble these four Jumbles, one letter
to each square, to form four ordinary words.

ARCTT

ESSOU

INJOAD

HISVAL

Sounds serious!

NOT THE SORT OF CASE
HE EXPECTED TO FIND
IN THE BUNGALOW.

Now arrange the circled letters to form
the surprise answer, as suggested by the
above cartoon.

Print answer here **A**

JUMBLE®

Unscramble these four Jumbles, one letter
to each square, to form four ordinary words.

CHENE

LIDEY

DRIPUT

MELFYS

WHAT THE
MILLIONAIRE
LEFT.

Now arrange the circled letters to form
the surprise answer, as suggested by the
above cartoon.

**Print
answer
here** ⬡⬡⬡⬡ TO BE ⬡⬡⬡⬡⬡⬡⬡⬡

JUMBLE®

Unscramble these four Jumbles, one letter
to each square, to form four ordinary words.

CUTOS

GANTY

LENZOZ

MOOGLY

Will you let me get a
word in edgewise?

WHAT A CONVER-
SATION BETWEEN
HUSBAND AND
WIFE SOMETIMES IS.

Now arrange the circled letters to form
the surprise answer, as suggested by the
above cartoon.

Print answer here A ◯◯◯◯◯◯◯◯◯◯

JUMBLE®

Unscramble these four Jumbles, one letter
to each square, to form four ordinary words.

TUMSY

GEESI

LIVERD

SLAPOT

CANDY

But you promised!

WHAT TEARS ARE.

Now arrange the circled letters to form
the surprise answer, as suggested by the
above cartoon.

Print answer here " ⬡⬡⬡⬡ " ⬡⬡⬡⬡⬡

JUMBLE®

Unscramble these four Jumbles, one letter
to each square, to form four ordinary words.

GREEM

NARCH

CAFFEE

TABMIG

OUR ANCESTORS

HOW SOME
PROMINENT
FAMILY TREES
WERE STARTED.

Now arrange the circled letters to form
the surprise answer, as suggested by the
above cartoon.

Print answer here BY " ⬡⬡⬡⬡⬡⬡⬡⬡⬡ "

JUMBLE®

Unscramble these four Jumbles, one letter
to each square, to form four ordinary words.

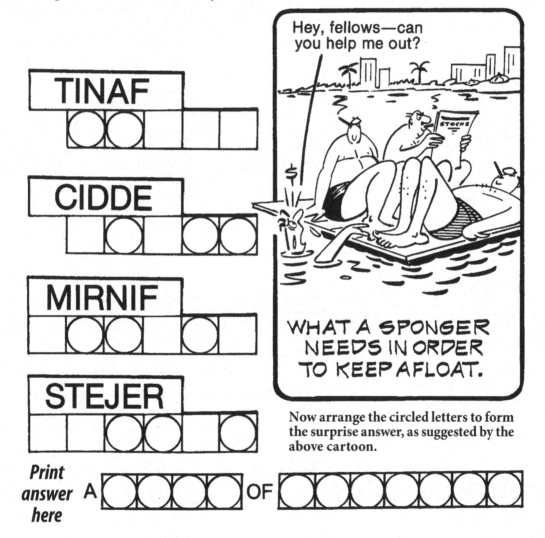

Hey, fellows—can
you help me out?

WHAT A SPONGER
NEEDS IN ORDER
TO KEEP AFLOAT.

TINAF

CIDDE

MIRNIF

STEJER

Now arrange the circled letters to form
the surprise answer, as suggested by the
above cartoon.

**Print
answer
here** A ⬡⬡⬡⬡ OF ⬡⬡⬡⬡⬡⬡⬡

JUMBLE®

Unscramble these four Jumbles, one letter to each square, to form four ordinary words.

DRECY

NACHT

RATYGE

HALVIS

Our new chairman

HOW THE BIG VOTE TURNED OUT AT THE OPTICIANS' CONVENTION.

Now arrange the circled letters to form the surprise answer, as suggested by the above cartoon.

Print answer here THE " ⬡⬡⬡⬡⬡ " ⬡⬡⬡IT

JUMBLE®

Unscramble these four Jumbles, one letter
to each square, to form four ordinary words.

MEPIR

BLEEL

EXFRIP

TRAMOF

THE ONLY THING HE
HAD AGAINST THE
YOUNGER GENER-
ATION WAS THAT
HE WAS NOT THIS.

Now arrange the circled letters to form
the surprise answer, as suggested by the
above cartoon.

Print answer here A ◯◯◯◯◯◯ ◯◯ IT

JUMBLE.

Unscramble these four Jumbles, one letter to each square, to form four ordinary words.

ROATA

BYDAN

PELETS

DEELEN

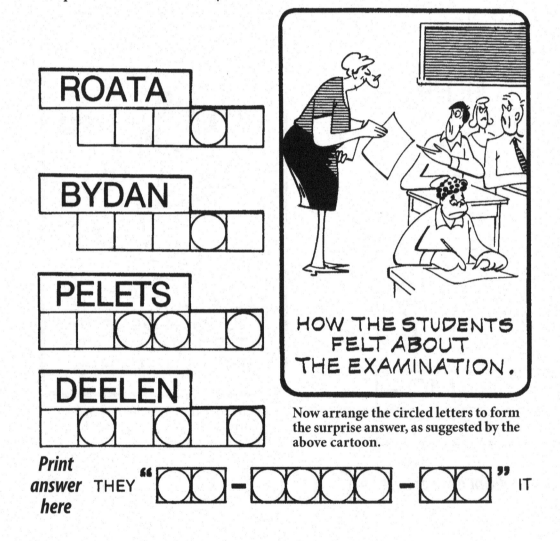

HOW THE STUDENTS FELT ABOUT THE EXAMINATION.

Now arrange the circled letters to form the surprise answer, as suggested by the above cartoon.

Print answer here THEY " ⬜⬜-⬜⬜⬜⬜-⬜⬜ " IT

JUMBLE®

Unscramble these four Jumbles, one letter
to each square, to form four ordinary words.

YASAS

TYPAR

GRUNNE

DAILIN

WHAT HE
QUIT DOING
IN TRYING TIMES.

Now arrange the circled letters to form
the surprise answer, as suggested by the
above cartoon.

Print answer here

JUMBLE®

Unscramble these four Jumbles, one letter
to each square, to form four ordinary words.

BOYTO

YAFOR

TREMIC

DEMPIN

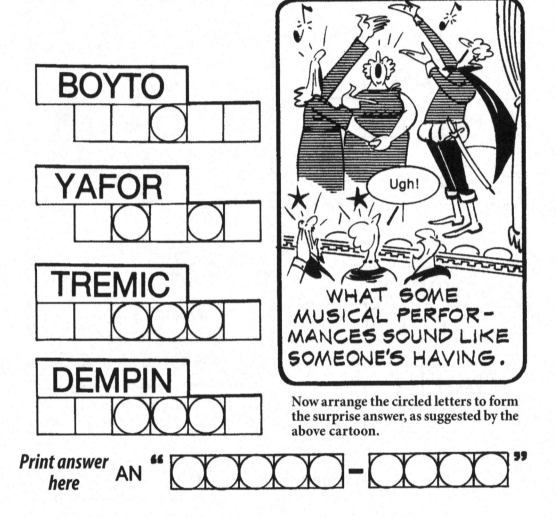

Ugh!

WHAT SOME
MUSICAL PERFOR-
MANCES SOUND LIKE
SOMEONE'S HAVING.

Now arrange the circled letters to form
the surprise answer, as suggested by the
above cartoon.

Print answer here AN " ◯◯◯◯◯ – ◯◯◯◯ "

JUMBLE®

Unscramble these four Jumbles, one letter
to each square, to form four ordinary words.

CALLI

ADDEJ

TERIAP

VINTER

Enjoy!

HE FELT THE ONLY
WAY TO MULTIPLY
HAPPINESS
WAS THIS.

Now arrange the circled letters to form
the surprise answer, as suggested by the
above cartoon.

Print answer here TO ☐☐☐☐☐☐ ☐☐

JUMBLE®

Unscramble these four Jumbles, one letter to each square, to form four ordinary words.

DRIAP

KIMPS

MADORR

LENKEN

WHAT HE SUFFERED FROM WHEN THE RELATIVES ARRIVED.

Now arrange the circled letters to form the surprise answer, as suggested by the above cartoon.

Print answer here "◯◯◯ – ◯◯◯◯◯◯"

JUMBLE®

Unscramble these four Jumbles, one letter
to each square, to form four ordinary words.

SATHY

HASAB

TAYRRM

SUPCAM

WHAT ANY GOOD
JUNKMAN KNOWS
HOW TO CONVERT.

Now arrange the circled letters to form
the surprise answer, as suggested by the
above cartoon.

**Print answer
here** ⬡⬡⬡⬡⬡ INTO ⬡⬡⬡⬡

JUMBLE®

Unscramble these four Jumbles, one letter
to each square, to form four ordinary words.

INLOG

YORRS

CUDINT

NERKUB

HE WAS SO
HEALTHY
IT WAS THIS.

Now arrange the circled letters to form
the surprise answer, as suggested by the
above cartoon.

Print answer **"**
here
"

JUMBLE®

Unscramble these four Jumbles, one letter
to each square, to form four ordinary words.

KNALB

ENKLE

FLUDON

TORFOG

BEGINNING HORSE-
BACK RIDERS OFTEN
DO IT THIS WAY.

Now arrange the circled letters to form
the surprise answer, as suggested by the
above cartoon.

Print answer here

JUMBLE®

Unscramble these four Jumbles, one letter
to each square, to form four ordinary words.

PROWE

PAKKO

LITGUY

QUIROL

SOME GIRLS
CLOSE THEIR EYES
WHILE KISSING, BUT
OTHERS DO THIS.

Now arrange the circled letters to form
the surprise answer, as suggested by the
above cartoon.

*Print answer
here* ☐◯◯◯◯☐ BEFORE " ◯◯◯ "
THEY

JUMBLE.

Unscramble these four Jumbles, one letter
to each square, to form four ordinary words.

TEGOB

ROBIT

INSHIF

PEWDOL

THAT AFTER-DINNER
SPEAKER ALWAYS
KNEW WHEN TO RISE
TO THE OCCASION —
BUT SELDOM THIS.

Now arrange the circled letters to form
the surprise answer, as suggested by the
above cartoon.

*Print answer
here* WHEN

JUMBLE®

Unscramble these four Jumbles, one letter
to each square, to form four ordinary words.

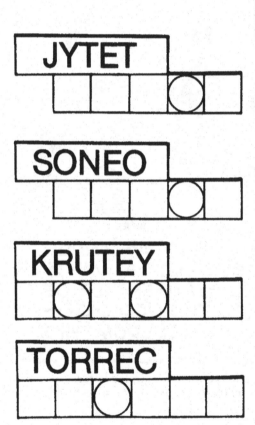

JYTET

SONEO

KRUTEY

TORREC

WHAT HE GOT
WHEN HE BOUGHT
THAT STOCK.

Now arrange the circled letters to form
the surprise answer, as suggested by the
above cartoon.

Print answer here

JUMBLE®

Unscramble these four Jumbles, one letter
to each square, to form four ordinary words.

TELIT

RADAW

RAYLEY

VIRFED

MILK

A CONFIRMED
NIGHT OWL IS A
MAN WHO STAYS
UP ALL NIGHT—

Now arrange the circled letters to form
the surprise answer, as suggested by the
above cartoon.

*Print
answer
here*

JUMBLE®

Unscramble these four Jumbles, one letter
to each square, to form four ordinary words.

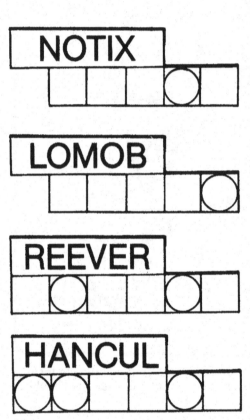

NOTIX

LOMOB

REEVER

HANCUL

IT'S SOMETIMES
A CRIME TO CATCH
FISH HERE, BUT
MORE OFTEN THIS.

Now arrange the circled letters to form
the surprise answer, as suggested by the
above cartoon.

Print answer here A

JUMBLE®

Unscramble these four Jumbles, one letter
to each square, to form four ordinary words.

SEBOE

VENOL

UNJAYT

LIMSAD

Get to work!

WHAT HIS WIFE
HAD A STEADY
JOB TRYING
TO KEEP HIM AT.

Now arrange the circled letters to form
the surprise answer, as suggested by the
above cartoon.

**Print answer
here** A ⊂⊃⊂⊃⊂⊃⊂⊃⊂⊃⊂⊃ ⊂⊃⊂⊃⊂⊃

JUMBLE®

Unscramble these four Jumbles, one letter
to each square, to form four ordinary words.

YURST

WHASS

UNEEVA

GREDLE

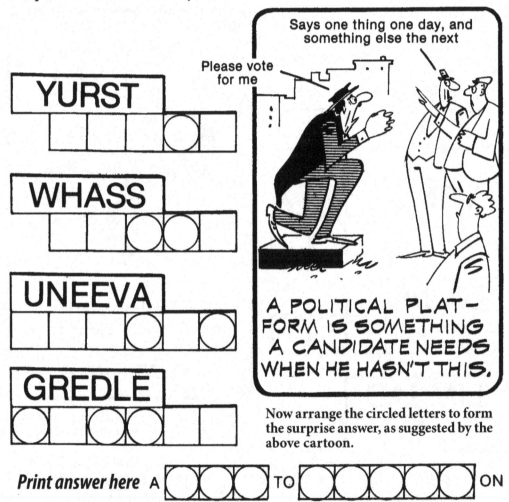

Please vote for me

Says one thing one day, and something else the next

A POLITICAL PLAT—
FORM IS SOMETHING
A CANDIDATE NEEDS
WHEN HE HASN'T THIS.

Now arrange the circled letters to form
the surprise answer, as suggested by the
above cartoon.

Print answer here A ⬡⬡⬡ TO ⬡⬡⬡⬡⬡ ON

JUMBLE®

Unscramble these four Jumbles, one letter
to each square, to form four ordinary words.

YOMSS

EUQUE

TAUMER

DEXOUS

AN IMPATIENT
DRIVER WHO
HAS TO STOP FOR
A TRAFFIC LIGHT
USUALLY DOES THIS.

Now arrange the circled letters to form
the surprise answer, as suggested by the
above cartoon.

Print answer here " ⬭⬭⬭⬭ ⬭⬭⬭ "

JUMBLE®

Unscramble these four Jumbles, one letter
to each square, to form four ordinary words.

NOWDY

VOACH

ANCIDD

BLOGIE

Disgraceful!

But interesting!

WHAT SCANDAL HAS TO BE.

Now arrange the circled letters to form
the surprise answer, as suggested by the
above cartoon.

Print answer here ⬡⬡⬡ TO BE ⬡⬡⬡⬡

JUMBLE®

Unscramble these four Jumbles, one letter
to each square, to form four ordinary words.

TOORB

PULIT

RECLEY

TORETT

THE BEST WAY TO
BETTER YOUR LOT
IS TO DO THIS.

Now arrange the circled letters to form
the surprise answer, as suggested by the
above cartoon.

Print answer here A ◯◯◯◯ ◯◯◯◯◯◯◯

JUMBLE®

Unscramble these four Jumbles, one letter
to each square, to form four ordinary words.

FYNAC

ARREM

LIDBOY

YESGER

HOW SOMEONE WHO
SOWED TOO MANY
WILD OATS WHEN HE
WAS YOUNG MIGHT
END UP LOOKING.

Now arrange the circled letters to form
the surprise answer, as suggested by the
above cartoon.

Print answer here "  "

JUMBLE®

Unscramble these four Jumbles, one letter
to each square, to form four ordinary words.

SLEHW

LIQUA

WELLOY

CROVAT

WHAT SORT OF
CONVERSATION
WAS GOING ON AT
THE LIBRARY?

Now arrange the circled letters to form
the surprise answer, as suggested by the
above cartoon.

Print answer here A ⬡⬡⬡⬡ " ⬡⬡⬡ " ONE

JUMBLE®

Unscramble these four Jumbles, one letter
to each square, to form four ordinary words.

KEHRI

EXVIN

TOBUNT

RAZTUQ

Yeah—I
remember when
they were
all born

ANOTHER NAME
FOR THAT
MUCH TALKED
ABOUT BABY BOOM.

Now arrange the circled letters to form
the surprise answer, as suggested by the
above cartoon.

*Print
answer
here* THE "⬡⬡⬡⬡⬡⬡⬡⬡⬡⬡⬡⬡"

JUMBLE®

Unscramble these four Jumbles, one letter to each square, to form four ordinary words.

GIRRO

ENVAH

NUIRJY

RUSTYD

OUCH!

A HANDY DEVICE FOR FINDING FURNITURE IN THE DARK.

Now arrange the circled letters to form the surprise answer, as suggested by the above cartoon.

Print answer here ⬡⬡⬡⬡ ⬡⬡⬡⬡

JUMBLE®

Unscramble these four Jumbles, one letter
to each square, to form four ordinary words.

CARTT

LALAM

NECCIS

SYTTUR

WHAT THOSE
OLD SAILING
-VESSELS MUST
HAVE PROVIDED.

Now arrange the circled letters to form
the surprise answer, as suggested by the
above cartoon.

**Print
answer
here**

JUMBLE.

Unscramble these four Jumbles, one letter to each square, to form four ordinary words.

CAMPH

SUROE

HERITH

BLUMFE

SNACKS MEANT
TO REFRESH
OFTEN END
UP DOING THIS.

Now arrange the circled letters to form the surprise answer, as suggested by the above cartoon.

Print answer here " ⬡⬡⬡⬡⬡⬡⬡ "

JUMBLE®

Unscramble these four Jumbles, one letter
to each square, to form four ordinary words.

YEASS

RINBY

KAMBER

PLOUCE

WHAT A PERSON
WHO BELIEVES
IN FORTUNE-
TELLERS MIGHT BE.

Now arrange the circled letters to form
the surprise answer, as suggested by the
above cartoon.

Print
answer A "⬡⬡⬡⬡" ⬡⬡⬡⬡⬡⬡⬡
here

JUMBLE®

Unscramble these four Jumbles, one letter to each square, to form four ordinary words.

RIHAC

ALMEY

YARTIF

DEXENP

Are you listening to all this?!

WHAT A STUFFED SHIRT OFTEN GOES WITH.

Now arrange the circled letters to form the surprise answer, as suggested by the above cartoon.

Print answer here AN ⬡⬡⬡⬡⬡ ⬡⬡⬡⬡

JUMBLE®

Unscramble these four Jumbles, one letter
to each square, to form four ordinary words.

RAFIR

SETTY

INTERE

LEMETH

What's the use of catching them?
They only get let off

SOMETIMES
A POLICE
DOG IS THE ONLY
LAW WITH THIS.

Now arrange the circled letters to form
the surprise answer, as suggested by the
above cartoon.

Print answer here

JUMBLE®

Unscramble these four Jumbles, one letter to each square, to form four ordinary words.

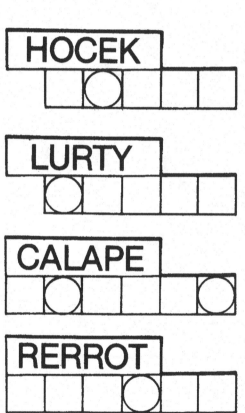

HOCEK

LURTY

CALAPE

RERROT

You can't beat buying land

REAL ESTATE

IT COULD BE THE BEST INVESTMENT ON EARTH!

Now arrange the circled letters to form the surprise answer, as suggested by the above cartoon.

Print answer here

JUMBLE®

Unscramble these four Jumbles, one letter
to each square, to form four ordinary words.

TOANB

POANI

KITSCY

GATHUC

WHEN DENTISTS
AREN'T, THEIR
PATIENTS ARE.

Now arrange the circled letters to form
the surprise answer, as suggested by the
above cartoon.

Print answer
here

JUMBLE®

Unscramble these four Jumbles, one letter to each square, to form four ordinary words.

REBLY

PLYAP

LETLIF

BROIMD

I'm thirsty

THE BEST WINE
AFTER A
LONG VOYAGE.

Now arrange the circled letters to form the surprise answer, as suggested by the above cartoon.

Print answer here

JUMBLE®

Unscramble these four Jumbles, one letter to each square, to form four ordinary words.

NILTE

HIRAY

NISUFE

PINGRY

THE PIANIST WAS A MUSICIAN TO THIS.

Now arrange the circled letters to form the surprise answer, as suggested by the above cartoon.

Print answer here HIS ⟨◯◯◯◯◯◯◯◯◯◯⟩

JUMBLE®

Unscramble these four Jumbles, one letter to each square, to form four ordinary words.

CHUVO

AUFAN

EXVONC

AREPPA

How ignorant can you get?

A PREJUDICED GUY IS DOWN ON ANYTHING HE'S NOT THIS.

Now arrange the circled letters to form the surprise answer, as suggested by the above cartoon.

Print answer here ⬭⬭ ⬭⬭

JUMBLE®

Unscramble these four Jumbles, one letter to each square, to form four ordinary words.

MAUSE

PAROE

JANGOR

NODARP

WHAT THE TUBA PLAYER'S KIDS CALLED HIM.

Now arrange the circled letters to form the surprise answer, as suggested by the above cartoon.

Print answer here " ☐☐☐ - ☐☐ - ☐☐ "

JUMBLE.

Unscramble these four Jumbles, one letter
to each square, to form four ordinary words.

RYFIA

BROAN

TRAGEY

NACUNE

WHAT THE FLAG
COMPANY HAD.

Now arrange the circled letters to form
the surprise answer, as suggested by the
above cartoon.

Print answer
here   A

JUMBLE®

Unscramble these four Jumbles, one letter
to each square, to form four ordinary words.

TYMUS

WILLT

GULJEG

TUSALE

Our dear uncle
told me I'll be
his sole heir!

That's
what he
told
me!

WHAT THE
FEUDING BROTHERS
FACED IN THE
INHERITANCE DISPUTE.

Now arrange the circled letters to form
the surprise answer, as suggested by the
above cartoon.

Print answer here A ⬡⬡⬡⬡⬡ OF ⬡⬡⬡⬡⬡⬡

JUMBLE®

Unscramble these four Jumbles, one letter to each square, to form four ordinary words.

DUJEG

FIBTE

MABGIT

FROMIN

I feel a lot better

HOW THE BODY BUILDER FELT AFTER A HAIRCUT.

Now arrange the circled letters to form the surprise answer, as suggested by the above cartoon.

Print answer here ⬡⬡⬡ AND ⬡⬡⬡⬡⬡⬡⬡

JUMBLE®

Unscramble these four Jumbles, one letter
to each square, to form four ordinary words.

MARRO

AKELY

NEDDAW

SELIVA

CAUTION
WHEN
WET

WHAT DRIVERS CALLED
THE SLIPPERY ROAD.

Now arrange the circled letters to form
the surprise answer, as suggested by the
above cartoon.

Print answer here

JUMBLE®

Unscramble these four Jumbles, one letter to each square, to form four ordinary words.

SNURP

FEMAL

TOLBET

PRONED

Your looks are gone—I'm replacing you

WHAT HAPPENED TO THE BALDING ACTOR?

Now arrange the circled letters to form the surprise answer, as suggested by the above cartoon.

Print answer here   HE ⟨◯◯◯◯⟩ HIS ⟨◯◯◯◯⟩

JUMBLE®

Unscramble these four Jumbles, one letter
to each square, to form four ordinary words.

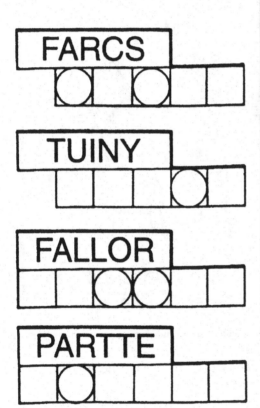

FARCS

TUINY

FALLOR

PARTTE

Lemme tell you about this bozo...

WHAT THE
GUEST OF HONOR
RECEIVED AT HIS
TESTIMONIAL DINNER.

Now arrange the circled letters to form
the surprise answer, as suggested by the
above cartoon.

Print answer here

JUMBLE®

Unscramble these four Jumbles, one letter
to each square, to form four ordinary words.

AFESH

ROCUS

SOUBLE

MORRET

When we finish, class, this
will be as good as new

WHERE HOME
REMODELERS LEARN
THEIR TRADE.

Now arrange the circled letters to form
the surprise answer, as suggested by the
above cartoon.

Print
answer AT "◯◯-◯◯◯◯◯" ◯◯◯◯◯◯
here

JUMBLE ®

Unscramble these four Jumbles, one letter to each square, to form four ordinary words.

GUNTS

GUAVE

HOCCUR

GARUJA

Those phones never stop!

WHAT THE SWITCH-
BOARD OPERATOR WAS
AT THE END
OF THE DAY.

Now arrange the circled letters to form the surprise answer, as suggested by the above cartoon.

Print answer here

JUMBLE®

Unscramble these four Jumbles, one letter
to each square, to form four ordinary words.

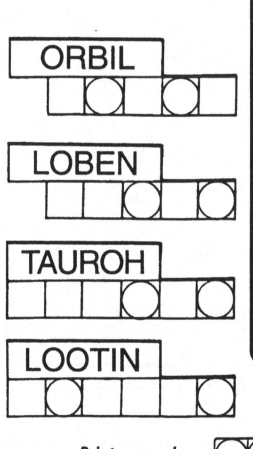

ORBIL

LOBEN

TAUROH

LOOTIN

He'll be a flier some day

With his own plane

WHEN THE RICH
PILOT'S SON ARRIVED
HE WAS----

Now arrange the circled letters to form
the surprise answer, as suggested by the
above cartoon.

Print answer here

JUMBLE®

Unscramble these four Jumbles, one letter
to each square, to form four ordinary words.

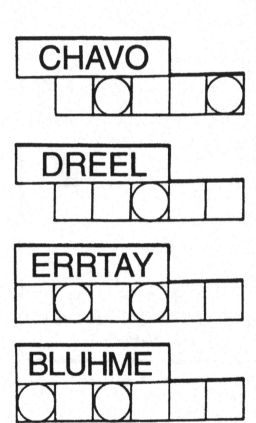

CHAVO

DREEL

ERRTAY

BLUHME

How does he do that?

THE KIND OF LIFE
SOME SNAKES LEAD.

Now arrange the circled letters to form
the surprise answer, as suggested by the
above cartoon.

Print answer here

JUMBLE®

Unscramble these four Jumbles, one letter
to each square, to form four ordinary words.

SNOBI

USIGE

MILIES

SHOPIN

It's all
yours

WHAT THE DONUT
BAKER GAVE HIS SON
WHEN HE RETIRED.

Now arrange the circled letters to form
the surprise answer, as suggested by the
above cartoon.

Print
answer   THE
here

JUMBLE®

Unscramble these four Jumbles, one letter to each square, to form four ordinary words.

MOROG

OPUCE

TUIFLE

MINOOT

Now be sure you call us

Why don't you ever trust me?!

WHERE CHILDREN SOMETIMES TRY TO SEND THEIR PARENTS.

Now arrange the circled letters to form the surprise answer, as suggested by the above cartoon.

Print answer here ON A ☐☐☐☐☐ ☐☐☐☐

JUMBLE®

Unscramble these four Jumbles, one letter
to each square, to form four ordinary words.

LUBLY

RUFOL

TALOZE

RUMMUR

Out!

WHAT THE TENNIS
PLAYER SAID WHEN
HE LOST THE GAME.

Now arrange the circled letters to form
the surprise answer, as suggested by the
above cartoon.

Print answer here " ☐☐ ☐☐☐☐☐ "

JUMBLE®

Unscramble these four Jumbles, one letter
to each square, to form four ordinary words.

SOUHE

DIEFT

PANICT

SHONCE

Here they are, chief

EDITOR

Just
in
time

THE CAMERAMAN
MET HIS NEWSPAPER
DEADLINE WITH THIS.

Now arrange the circled letters to form
the surprise answer, as suggested by the
above cartoon.

Print answer
here   A

JUMBLE®

Unscramble these four Jumbles, one letter
to each square, to form four ordinary words.

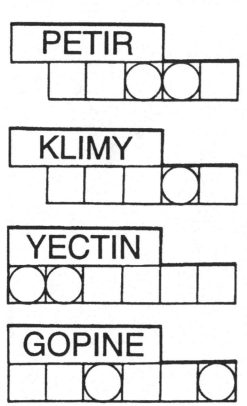

PETIR

KLIMY

YECTIN

GOPINE

Very good

WHAT THE MONARCH
USED ON THE
NEWBORN HEIR.

Now arrange the circled letters to form
the surprise answer, as suggested by the
above cartoon.

Print answer here A

JUMBLE®

Unscramble these four Jumbles, one letter
to each square, to form four ordinary words.

TOSOP

CLATH

SWACHE

PINTUR

This should give us all
a good time

ALWAYS SOUGHT
BUT NEVER BOUGHT.

Now arrange the circled letters to form
the surprise answer, as suggested by the
above cartoon.

Print answer here

JUMBLE®

Unscramble these four Jumbles, one letter
to each square, to form four ordinary words.

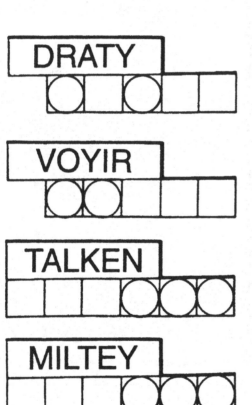

DRATY

VOYIR

TALKEN

MILTEY

'Bye, Grandma

WHAT SOME
LEAVE BEHIND
WHEN GETTING AWAY
FROM IT ALL.

Now arrange the circled letters to form
the surprise answer, as suggested by the
above cartoon.

Print answer here

JUMBLE®

Unscramble these four Jumbles, one letter
to each square, to form four ordinary words.

ADDIE

MOURF

MENECT

LEWOLF

Bill Hanson! I haven't
seen you since we
dated in school!

Mary!

WHAT THE FIRE
INSPECTOR DISCOVERED.

Now arrange the circled letters to form
the surprise answer, as suggested by the
above cartoon.

Print answer here AN

JUMBLE®

Unscramble these four Jumbles, one letter
to each square, to form four ordinary words.

VELDE

BAXOR

YEMBOR

ELYSEP

How much can you lift?

WHAT THE WEIGHT-
LIFTER FOUND AT
HIS FAVORITE HANGOUT.

Now arrange the circled letters to form
the surprise answer, as suggested by the
above cartoon.

Print answer here

JUMBLE®

Unscramble these four Jumbles, one letter
to each square, to form four ordinary words.

REEMY

RABDN

GLERCY

NAIFEL

SOMETHING HE GOT
WHEN HE JOINED
THE KNITTING CLASS.

Now arrange the circled letters to form
the surprise answer, as suggested by the
above cartoon.

Print answer here THE

JUMBLE®

Unscramble these four Jumbles, one letter
to each square, to form four ordinary words.

EHITT

EGOYO

SNENUE

TARRMY

THE HORSE WITH THE
OVERLY NEGATIVE
ATTITUDE
WAS A ---

Now arrange the circled letters to form
the surprise answer, as suggested by the
above cartoon.

Print
answer
here

" ⬡⬡⬡⬡⬡ - ⬡⬡⬡⬡⬡ "

JUMBLE®

Unscramble these four Jumbles, one letter
to each square, to form four ordinary words.

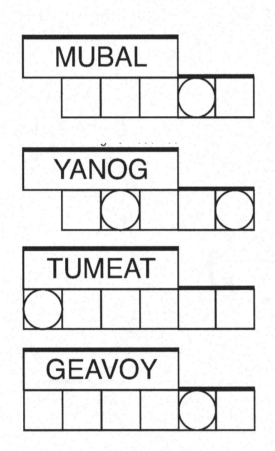

MUBAL

YANOG

TUMEAT

GEAVOY

I think I'm
overdressed
for in here.

I lost five
pounds today.

JUMBLE
JAVA

EVEN THOUGH IT WAS
COLD AND DRY OUTSIDE,
INSIDE THE COFFEE SHOP
IT WAS ----

Now arrange the circled letters to form
the surprise answer, as suggested by the
above cartoon.

Print answer here

JUMBLE®

Unscramble these four Jumbles, one letter to each square, to form four ordinary words.

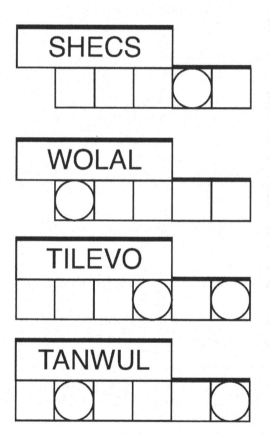

SHECS

WOLAL

TILEVO

TANWUL

FINISH

Way to go!

I can't believe I finally did it!

AFTER ATTEMPTING TO WIN FOR YEARS, HE FINISHED FIRST ---

Now arrange the circled letters to form the surprise answer, as suggested by the above cartoon.

 Print answer here

JUMBLE®

Unscramble these four Jumbles, one letter
to each square, to form four ordinary words.

FIWST

GEODD

CIASOL

LEOPRA

Hi, everybody!
I hope you're
having a great
day!

How
wonderful
to see you,
Casper.

ALL THE OTHER GHOSTS
ENJOYED BEING WITH
CASPER BECAUSE HE WAS
ALWAYS IN ----

Now arrange the circled letters to form
the surprise answer, as suggested by the
above cartoon.

Print
answer
here

JUMBLE®

Unscramble these four Jumbles, one letter to each square, to form four ordinary words.

WRANP

GIHEW

COSTEK

GRAITU

I hear this place is great!

It better be.

Le Jumble BISTRO

THE POPULARITY OF THE RESTAURANT RESULTED IN CUSTOMERS BECOMING ----

Now arrange the circled letters to form the surprise answer, as suggested by the above cartoon.

Print answer here ⬡⬡⬡⬡⬡⬡⬡

JUMBLE®

Unscramble these four Jumbles, one letter to each square, to form four ordinary words.

REMHY

BORTO

DESEPY

SNAHIB

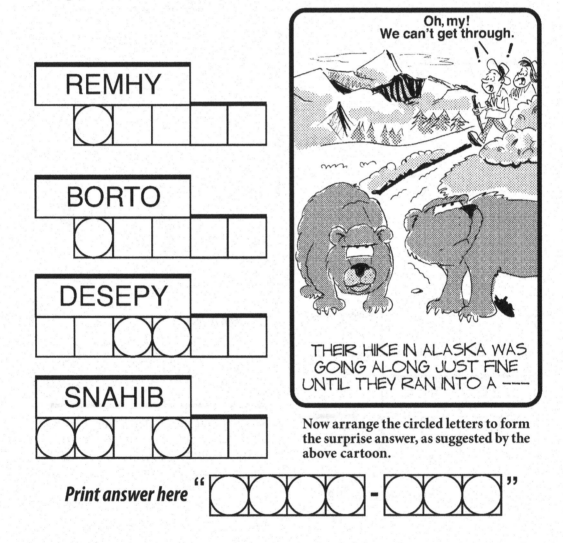

Oh, my! We can't get through.

THEIR HIKE IN ALASKA WAS GOING ALONG JUST FINE UNTIL THEY RAN INTO A ----

Now arrange the circled letters to form the surprise answer, as suggested by the above cartoon.

Print answer here " ◯◯◯◯ - ◯◯◯ "

JUMBLE®

Unscramble these four Jumbles, one letter
to each square, to form four ordinary words.

SCUMI

DEAGA

RABLER

TEGRUT

How can it be 7:15?
I thought I set the
clock for 6:00.
Sorry about that.

I'll be fine.
Traffic isn't so
horrible on
Wednesday.

SHE WOKE UP LATE,
BUT SHE WASN'T THIS.

Now arrange the circled letters to form
the surprise answer, as suggested by the
above cartoon.

Print answer here

JUMBLE®

Unscramble these four Jumbles, one letter to each square, to form four ordinary words.

MUGOB

SUMIN

TRYTEP

HEBDIN

AFTER YEARS WITHOUT STRIKING, THE PICKETERS HAD A ----

Now arrange the circled letters to form the surprise answer, as suggested by the above cartoon.

Print answer here ◯◯ - ◯◯◯◯◯

JUMBLE®

Unscramble these four Jumbles, one letter
to each square, to form four ordinary words.

RANEA

DRANG

TIMCER

ABENTE

WELCOME BUTCHERS!

Hi. I'm Sam.

The name's Ed.

So, Tom, what's your favorite cut?

THE BUTCHERS'
CONVENTION FEATURED
A _ _ _

Now arrange the circled letters to form
the surprise answer, as suggested by the
above cartoon.

Print answer here " ◯◯◯◯ " ◯◯◯ ◯◯◯◯◯

JUMBLE®

Unscramble these four Jumbles, one letter
to each square, to form four ordinary words.

VERIR

NONIO

KRUTEY

WEHAIL

COMING SOON
Fishers Fitness

I'm sorry, but my crew went on strike.

Well, that's not good. But I'm sure we'll still open on time.

CONSTRUCTION ON THE NEW GYM WASN'T GOING WELL, BUT EVERYTHING WOULD ----

Now arrange the circled letters to form
the surprise answer, as suggested by the
above cartoon.

Print answer here

JUMBLE®

Unscramble these four Jumbles, one letter to each square, to form four ordinary words.

NOUGY

RIWEP

DORSUH

PUTBAR

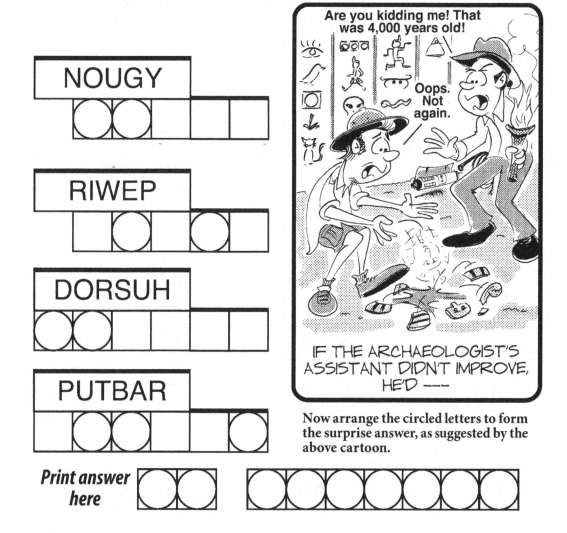

Are you kidding me! That was 4,000 years old!

Oops. Not again.

IF THE ARCHAEOLOGIST'S ASSISTANT DIDN'T IMPROVE, HE'D ———

Now arrange the circled letters to form the surprise answer, as suggested by the above cartoon.

Print answer here

JUMBLE®

Unscramble these four Jumbles, one letter
to each square, to form four ordinary words.

RUNPS

PIMKS

BUPCIL

NEPHHY

I picked another couple dozen ears for you.

WHEN SHE REALIZED HOW
LONG IT WOULD TAKE TO
REMOVE ALL THE CORN
HUSKS, SHE SAID ---

Now arrange the circled letters to form
the surprise answer, as suggested by the
above cartoon.

Print answer here

JUMBLE®

Unscramble these four Jumbles, one letter to each square, to form four ordinary words.

SEGUT

LETSY

TURAGI

TOMINO

I bought some swampland. I'm going to build on it.

I've been investing my 401k into high tech. It's really taken off.

BIG BIRD WASN'T WORRIED ABOUT RETIREMENT BECAUSE HE HAD A ---

Now arrange the circled letters to form the surprise answer, as suggested by the above cartoon.

Print answer here

JUMBLE®

Unscramble these four Jumbles, one letter
to each square, to form four ordinary words.

GIRNB

NIBOS

NOCMUL

URUYXL

Now, let's convert these
temperatures from
Farenheit to Celsius.

32=
89=
102=

I hope they
send us
home.

I can't
feel my
hands!

AFTER THE HEAT WENT OUT
IN THE SCHOOL, THE MATH
CLASS FEATURED ----

Now arrange the circled letters to form
the surprise answer, as suggested by the
above cartoon.

Print answer " ☐◯◯◯◯ - ☐◯◯◯◯◯ "
here

JUMBLE®

Unscramble these four Jumbles, one letter
to each square, to form four ordinary words.

MAYFO

CHEBA

GINISD

TEBLOT

Is this thing
big enough for
the both of
us?

My
ship!

HE WAS STRANDED AT
SEA, AND HIS BUDDY
WAS ---

Now arrange the circled letters to form
the surprise answer, as suggested by the
above cartoon.

**Print
answer
here**

JUMBLE®

Unscramble these four Jumbles, one letter to each square, to form four ordinary words.

PURUS

SAAIL

TEMRAT

NAYCON

LEVI STRAUSS & CO.

Overall, sales have been "riveting."

Levi, you're a "jeanius!"

LEVI STRAUSS' SUCCESS SELLING DENIM JEANS WAS A RESULT OF HIM BEING A ----

Now arrange the circled letters to form the surprise answer, as suggested by the above cartoon.

Print answer here

⟨ ⟩⟨ ⟩⟨ ⟩⟨ ⟩⟨ ⟩⟨ ⟩ - ⟨ ⟩⟨ ⟩⟨ ⟩⟨ ⟩⟨ ⟩

JUMBLE®

Unscramble these four Jumbles, one letter
to each square, to form four ordinary words.

MAIDT

MUTPH

ROCCEE

TOMRIP

Hey! This is not
the one I wanted.
It's not even a
real diamond!

But it cost
a lot less!

WHEN HE DIDN'T BUY
HIS WIFE THE DIAMOND
RING SHE WAS HOPING
FOR, HE ----

Now arrange the circled letters to form
the surprise answer, as suggested by the
above cartoon.

**Print
answer
here**

JUMBLE®

Unscramble these four Jumbles, one letter
to each square, to form four ordinary words.

RAPOE

PYGPU

FEDSUE

GARFOE

Wow!

THEIR VIEW OF THE
GRAND CANYON
WAS ---

Now arrange the circled letters to form
the surprise answer, as suggested by the
above cartoon.

Print answer " ◯◯◯◯◯ - ◯◯◯◯ "
here

JUMBLE®

Unscramble these four Jumbles, one letter to each square, to form four ordinary words.

WETIN

PEWST

PORYTH

RADELY

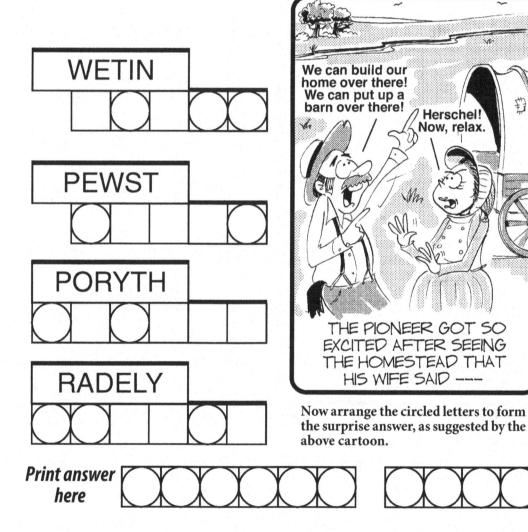

We can build our home over there! We can put up a barn over there!

Herschel! Now, relax.

THE PIONEER GOT SO EXCITED AFTER SEEING THE HOMESTEAD THAT HIS WIFE SAID ---

Now arrange the circled letters to form the surprise answer, as suggested by the above cartoon.

Print answer here

JUMBLE.

Unscramble these four Jumbles, one letter to each square, to form four ordinary words.

LADMY

DUMON

ONASCI

EPPPUT

TO HONOR WWII'S HEROES, ARCHITECT FRIEDRICH ST. FLORIAN CAME UP WITH AN IDEA THAT WAS ---

Now arrange the circled letters to form the surprise answer, as suggested by the above cartoon.

Print answer here

JUMBLE®

Unscramble these four Jumbles, one letter
to each square, to form four ordinary words.

GAMEO

TARAP

NOPVER

SUCOIN

Rise and shine! The crowd has gathered for your speech.

Oh, my back! The ground was so hard. I'm staying in a hotel tonight.

THE POLITICIAN HAD NEVER
SLEPT IN A TENT AND
DIDN'T LIKE THE ----

Now arrange the circled letters to form
the surprise answer, as suggested by the
above cartoon.

Print answer " ☐☐☐☐ - ☐☐☐☐ "
here

JUMBLE®

Unscramble these four Jumbles, one letter to each square, to form four ordinary words.

VEOCT

NIXTO

WARLPS

VODURE

It's here in the window so everyone can see it. Time to clean the glass.

I can't eat that! It's been in the sun too long.

SHE COULDN'T EAT HER PRIZE TOMATO BECAUSE IT HAD BEEN ---

Now arrange the circled letters to form the surprise answer, as suggested by the above cartoon.

Print answer here

⬡⬡⬡⬡⬡⬡⬡⬡ ⬡⬡⬡⬡⬡⬡

JUMBLE®

Unscramble these four Jumbles, one letter to each square, to form four ordinary words.

RONHO

ACCOO

BBOONH

MOYLOG

WHEN THE OWL
REALIZED HE WAS A
GHOST, HE SAID ----

Now arrange the circled letters to form the surprise answer, as suggested by the above cartoon.

Print answer here ◯◯◯ - ◯◯◯

JUMBLE®

Unscramble these four Jumbles, one letter
to each square, to form four ordinary words.

MOSTP

DEEWG

GHARNA

OPURTO

I just had to
get away
from Timmy
and all his
whining.

Well, no humans
here. We're our
own masters.

LASSIE BOUGHT THE
HOUSE BECAUSE THE
NEIGHBORHOOD HAD – – –

Now arrange the circled letters to form
the surprise answer, as suggested by the
above cartoon.

Print
answer
here

JUMBLE®

Unscramble these four Jumbles, one letter
to each square, to form four ordinary words.

ORCUC

SRAHH

MANEBO

STECKH

No charge.
It's what
we do.

I didn't know we were
getting a new roof too!
What do we owe you?

HELPFUL
HOMES

THERE WAS NO CHARGE
FOR THE SHINGLES
BECAUSE THEY WERE ---

Now arrange the circled letters to form
the surprise answer, as suggested by the
above cartoon.

Print
answer
here

JUMBLE®

Unscramble these four Jumbles, one letter
to each square, to form four ordinary words.

TINYU

ODIVE

CITILE

SIFLAC

We want to
get it fully
insured.

It's been in our family
for generations. We'll
leave it to our children.

It's
exquisite.

THEY GOT THE PAINTING
APPRAISED BECAUSE
THEY ----

Now arrange the circled letters to form
the surprise answer, as suggested by the
above cartoon.

Print answer
here

JUMBLE®

Unscramble these four Jumbles, one letter
to each square, to form four ordinary words.

VOABE

GANTW

NNALID

MURAAT

He could
take me into
custody
anytime.

I wish he were
looking for me.

Gotcha!

THE HANDSOME
BOUNTY HUNTER
WAS A ---

Now arrange the circled letters to form
the surprise answer, as suggested by the
above cartoon.

Print answer
here

JUMBLE®

Unscramble these four Jumbles, one letter to each square, to form four ordinary words.

AVEEW

TLOAT

CHROCS

SNENUK

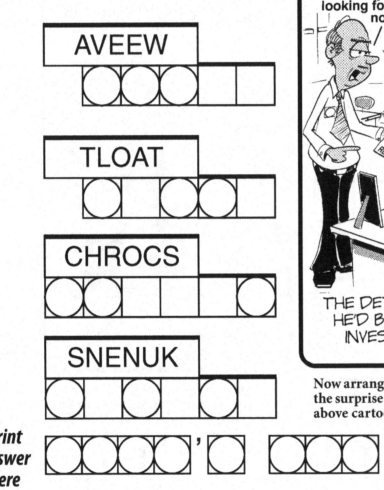

Give me the file you have on the mayor. You'll be looking for Mr. Puffy now.

What!? A lost cat?! I thought I was in charge of that investigation.

MISSING CAT REWARD

THE DETECTIVE THOUGHT HE'D BE HANDLING THE INVESTIGATION, BUT THAT ———

Now arrange the circled letters to form the surprise answer, as suggested by the above cartoon.

Print answer here

◯◯◯◯'◯ ◯◯◯ ◯◯◯◯

JUMBLE®

Unscramble these four Jumbles, one letter
to each square, to form four ordinary words.

NERAA

CITHH

OTBMTO

VALGER

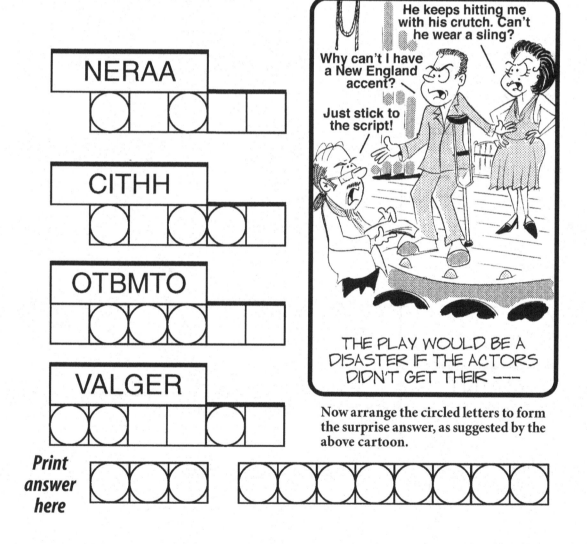

He keeps hitting me
with his crutch. Can't
he wear a sling?

Why can't I have
a New England
accent?

Just stick to
the script!

THE PLAY WOULD BE A
DISASTER IF THE ACTORS
DIDN'T GET THEIR ----

Now arrange the circled letters to form
the surprise answer, as suggested by the
above cartoon.

Print
answer
here

JUMBLE®

Unscramble these four Jumbles, one letter
to each square, to form four ordinary words.

OGDDE

VEARB

DURONA

CAINTT

What's the use? I'm outta here!

You can't quit! I quit!

I'm beating it.

THE ROCK GROUP WAS SO
BAD THAT THE AUDIENCE
LEFT. THEY WERE ----

Now arrange the circled letters to form
the surprise answer, as suggested by the
above cartoon.

Print answer here " ☐-☐☐☐☐-☐☐☐☐ "

JUMBLE®

Unscramble these four Jumbles, one letter to each square, to form four ordinary words.

YLSYH

SETGU

LASIVU

NOFDEF

Mac King
Comedy Magic
$7.99 Buffet

What do you mean you're broke?

I lost big!

CASINO

WHEN HE BLEW ALL HIS MONEY PLAYING SLOT MACHINES, POKER, ETC., HE WAS IN ----

Now arrange the circled letters to form the surprise answer, as suggested by the above cartoon.

Print answer " ◯◯◯◯ " ◯◯◯◯◯
here

JUMBLE®

Unscramble these four Jumbles, one letter
to each square, to form four ordinary words.

ROGMO

WONOS

SOMTED

CEBRIK

It's my best vinaigrette yet.

OK. We'll add it to today's show.

THE TV CHEF CAME UP WITH
THE NEW SALAD CONCEPT
IN HER ---

Now arrange the circled letters to form
the surprise answer, as suggested by the
above cartoon.

*Print
answer
here*

JUMBLE®

Unscramble these four Jumbles, one letter to each square, to form four ordinary words.

CAKOL

NIRKD

MEVORE

PIMKSY

Is it sturdy?

A volcano blast couldn't topple it.

BEFORE SIGNING THE CONTRACT FOR THE STONE HOME, HE WANTED TO MAKE SURE IT WAS ---

Now arrange the circled letters to form the surprise answer, as suggested by the above cartoon.

Print answer here ⬭⬭⬭⬭ - ⬭⬭⬭⬭⬭

JUMBLE®

Unscramble these four Jumbles, one letter
to each square, to form four ordinary words.

CLIER

SETLY

SELUFU

TROWDA

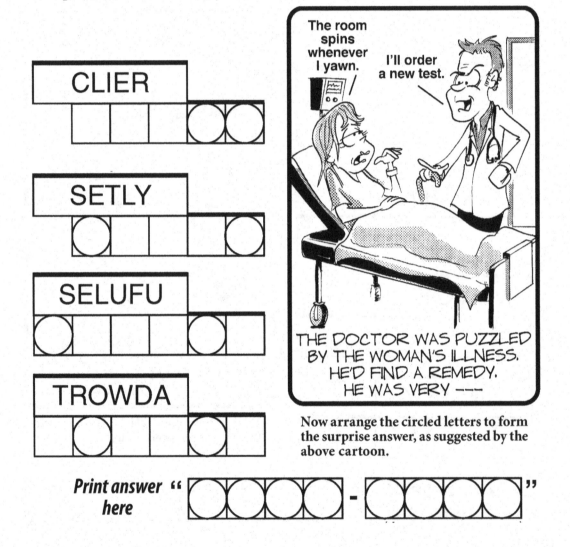

The room
spins
whenever
I yawn.

I'll order
a new test.

THE DOCTOR WAS PUZZLED
BY THE WOMAN'S ILLNESS.
HE'D FIND A REMEDY.
HE WAS VERY ———

Now arrange the circled letters to form
the surprise answer, as suggested by the
above cartoon.

Print answer "◯◯◯◯ - ◯◯◯◯"
here

JUMBLE®

Unscramble these four Jumbles, one letter
to each square, to form four ordinary words.

GIWEH

SOMEO

BILAVE

LUURYN

The fireplace sold us on this place.

It's so cozy.

Everyone's been so nice!

This is for you.

THE FIREPLACE IN THEIR NEW
HOME MADE FOR A NICE ----

Now arrange the circled letters to form
the surprise answer, as suggested by the
above cartoon.

Print
answer
here

JUMBLE®

Unscramble these four Jumbles, one letter to each square, to form four ordinary words.

RUPEN

GREEM

KINSYT

MERTAT

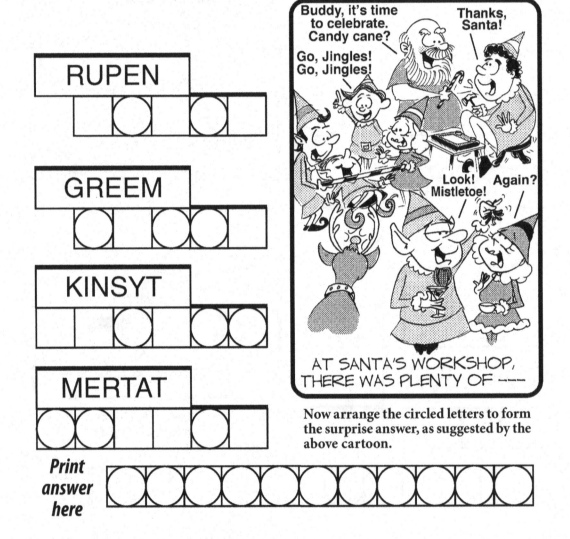

Buddy, it's time to celebrate. Candy cane?

Thanks, Santa!

Go, Jingles! Go, Jingles!

Look! Mistletoe!

Again?

AT SANTA'S WORKSHOP, THERE WAS PLENTY OF ---

Now arrange the circled letters to form the surprise answer, as suggested by the above cartoon.

Print answer here

JUMBLE®

Unscramble these four Jumbles, one letter
to each square, to form four ordinary words.

CHAWT

NUROD

CANMEE

TAUDEP

How dare you!
Look at this! You
kids today have
no respect.

Geez. Lighten up.
It lost its flavor.

AFTER SPITTING OUT HIS
BUBBLE GUM ON THE
SIDEWALK, THE TEEN
WAS ---

Now arrange the circled letters to form
the surprise answer, as suggested by the
above cartoon.

Print answer
here

JUMBLE®

Unscramble these four Jumbles, one letter to each square, to form four ordinary words.

LIHWE

CAQUK

COYKJE

TALAFO

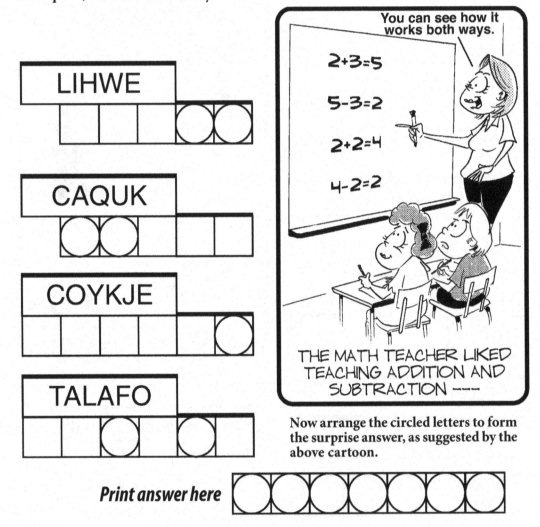

You can see how it works both ways.

2+3=5

5-3=2

2+2=4

4-2=2

THE MATH TEACHER LIKED TEACHING ADDITION AND SUBTRACTION ----

Now arrange the circled letters to form the surprise answer, as suggested by the above cartoon.

Print answer here

JUMBLE®

Unscramble these four Jumbles, one letter
to each square, to form four ordinary words.

CITDH

GUEOG

SOLIFS

GALGEG

So, what can we expect tomorrow?

Well, we usually just guess.

ASKED IF THERE'D BE
MORNING MIST, THE
WEATHERMAN DIDN'T
HAVE THE ---

Now arrange the circled letters to form
the surprise answer, as suggested by the
above cartoon.

*Print
answer
here*

JUMBLE®

Unscramble these four Jumbles, one letter to each square, to form four ordinary words.

CLEEX

TAPRA

LICCIN

TONKYT

I don't want any of those fancy "Cat Scams."

Is he even old enough to practice? I want Doc Johnson.

We'll have to give him a chance.

THE DOCTOR WOULD EVENTUALLY FEEL AT HOME IN THE NEW TOWN, IF HE HAD ENOUGH ----

Now arrange the circled letters to form the surprise answer, as suggested by the above cartoon.

Print answer here

JUMBLE®

Unscramble these four Jumbles, one letter
to each square, to form four ordinary words.

KEEOV

LIHDC

YREGSE

NOHHOC

HAPPY NEW YEAR

Here's
to 2016!

This
is
fun!

WHEN THEY TOASTED AT
THE NEW YEAR'S EVE PARTY,
EVERYONE WAS ———

Now arrange the circled letters to form
the surprise answer, as suggested by the
above cartoon.

*Print
answer
here* " "

JUMBLE®

Unscramble these four Jumbles, one letter to each square, to form four ordinary words.

MIREG

SMYES

NIBETT

GAVEOY

With all your aces today, I'll bet you're hungry.

This is perfect.

AFTER PLAYING TENNIS ALL DAY, HE WAS HAPPY FOR A MEAL WITH ---

Now arrange the circled letters to form the surprise answer, as suggested by the above cartoon.

Print answer here

JUMBLE®

Unscramble these four Jumbles, one letter to each square, to form four ordinary words.

GUHDO

PUSOY

ROWAND

SNUTUJ

Let me change that mic. It's picking up too much static.

Here you go.

IN TODAY'S HEADLINES, JUMBLE CREATOR WIN NOBEL

WHEN THE PRODUCER TOLD HIM HE NEEDED TO SWITCH MICROPHONES, HE SAID ----

Now arrange the circled letters to form the surprise answer, as suggested by the above cartoon.

Print answer here

JUMBLE®

Unscramble these four Jumbles, one letter to each square, to form four ordinary words.

SEETA

LEIRC

LEHDOB

ALCMYM

Wow! This is the coolest basement ever!

This is what a successful book gets you.

THE AUTHOR WHO WROTE FROM HIS BASEMENT HAD A ----

Now arrange the circled letters to form the surprise answer, as suggested by the above cartoon.

Print answer here

"   "

JUMBLE®

Unscramble these four Jumbles, one letter to each square, to form four ordinary words.

ZARRO

RIHYA

LIFEBE

TALCET

Traffic was horrible. It took 90 minutes to go 20 miles.

I only have a five-minute walk.

HOSPITAL

THE CARDIOLOGIST WAS ABLE TO WALK TO WORK BECAUSE HE LIVED IN THE ---

Now arrange the circled letters to form the surprise answer, as suggested by the above cartoon.

Print answer here

  THE

JUMBLE®

Unscramble these four Jumbles, one letter
to each square, to form four ordinary words.

ALUQI

DYDLO

DRAWYT

NAGCEH

Would you like
some more
coffee?

No thanks.
I'm late.

SLEEPY HOLLOW'S
HORSEMAN HAD FINISHED
BREAKFAST AND WAS
READY TO ---

Now arrange the circled letters to form
the surprise answer, as suggested by the
above cartoon.

Print answer here ◯◯◯◯ ◯◯◯

JUMBLE®

Unscramble these four Jumbles, one letter
to each square, to form four ordinary words.

GROCA

TNNIH

CEPTID

KEEUAR

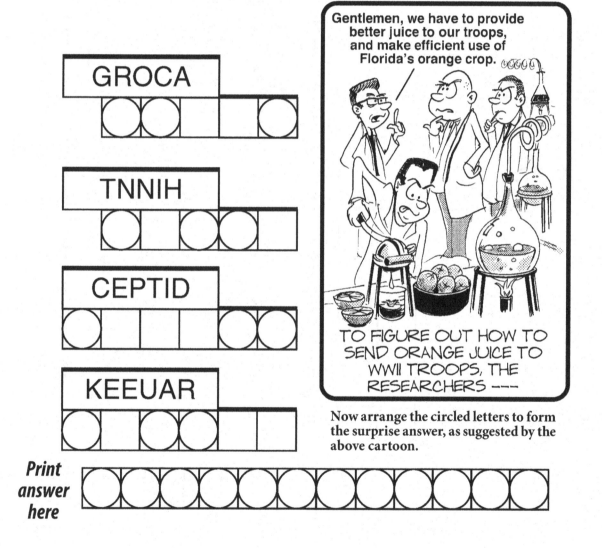

Gentlemen, we have to provide
better juice to our troops,
and make efficient use of
Florida's orange crop.

TO FIGURE OUT HOW TO
SEND ORANGE JUICE TO
WWII TROOPS, THE
RESEARCHERS ----

Now arrange the circled letters to form
the surprise answer, as suggested by the
above cartoon.

Print
answer
here

JUMBLE®

Unscramble these four Jumbles, one letter
to each square, to form four ordinary words.

SOGEO

SRAHH

ONVERP

SCAPUM

A decaf and
some hand
disinfectant.

WITH SO MANY CAPPUCCINO
AND LATTE DRINKERS
HAVING BAD COLDS, THE
CAFÉ WAS A ----

Now arrange the circled letters to form
the surprise answer, as suggested by the
above cartoon.

*Print
answer
here* "◯◯◯◯◯◯-◯◯" ◯◯◯◯

JUMBLE

Unscramble these four Jumbles, one letter
to each square, to form four ordinary words.

CITDH

VAROB

GANMEA

CLARIG

Why don't you
learn to dig a
proper hole? And
why don't you visit
your mother?

Why don't
you give it a
rest?

THE WEASEL DIDN'T LIKE HIS
PUSHY COUSIN BECAUSE HIS
COUSIN LIKED TO ---

Now arrange the circled letters to form
the surprise answer, as suggested by the
above cartoon.

**Print answer
here**

JUMBLE®

Unscramble these four Jumbles, one letter to each square, to form four ordinary words.

ELHOL

CRIBH

FISXUF

DOUHRS

Should I even bother plugging you in?

I can't even play a G.

AN ELECTRIC GUITAR WITH JUST ONE STRING IS ---

Now arrange the circled letters to form the surprise answer, as suggested by the above cartoon.

Print answer " ◯◯◯◯◯◯◯◯◯ "
here

162

JUMBLE Geography

Challenger Puzzles

JUMBLE®

Unscramble these six Jumbles, one letter to each square, to form six ordinary words.

MUFOSA

ENGALT

CURDEE

MIRTHE

LOMYEH

PETUCA

Wow! You're quick. Is everyone as nice as you here in Mexico?

It's my pleasure to help a beautiful lady like yourself.

AFTER THE WIND BLEW THE SOMBRERO OFF HER HEAD, HE PICKED IT UP FOR HER ———

Now arrange the circled letters to form the surprise answer, as suggested by the above cartoon.

Print answer here

JUMBLE®

Unscramble these six Jumbles, one letter to each square, to form six ordinary words.

GANEMA

OLFATA

CRENTH

HELAIN

CLABOT

RUFINA

This is such a great program for kids!

Wow! What a hit!

WHEN LITTLE LEAGUE BASEBALL WAS CREATED IN 1939, IT WAS POPULAR WITH PLAYERS AND FANS ----

Now arrange the circled letters to form the surprise answer, as suggested by the above cartoon.

Print answer here

JUMBLE®

Unscramble these six Jumbles, one letter
to each square, to form six ordinary words.

PRIZEP

BARRHO

NACCHE

TENTIK

SAUYEN

DERTNY

So, how is your son doing at college?

He's doing great. What about your daughter? Has she picked a major yet?

THEY JUMPED OUT OF
THE PLANE TOGETHER AND
WERE ABLE TO ----

Now arrange the circled letters to form
the surprise answer, as suggested by the
above cartoon.

Print answer here

" ⬭⬭⬭⬭⬭ " ⬭⬭⬭ ⬭⬭⬭⬭⬭⬭⬭

JUMBLE®

Unscramble these six Jumbles, one letter to each square, to form six ordinary words.

GIRPNS

SDERWH

FARDIA

UNATBE

SEWFET

RABKME

Ever since I was a young lad, I've wanted to climb to the summit.

It's fascinated me, too. We'll do it together.

HE DECIDED TO CLIMB MOUNT EVEREST BECAUSE THE WORLD'S TALLEST MOUNTAIN ----

Now arrange the circled letters to form the surprise answer, as suggested by the above cartoon.

Print answer here

" ⭕⭕⭕⭕⭕⭕ " ⭕⭕⭕ ⭕⭕⭕⭕⭕⭕⭕⭕⭕

JUMBLE®

Unscramble these six Jumbles, one letter to each square, to form six ordinary words.

SAWHEC

RETEWT

RARECE

WYLOLS

CUPKAN

VHSAIL

WHEN IT CAME TO WHICH NEW WINDOWS TO BUY, THE ---

Now arrange the circled letters to form the surprise answer, as suggested by the above cartoon.

Print answer here

JUMBLE®

Unscramble these six Jumbles, one letter to each square, to form six ordinary words.

TERERV

RUILOQ

AKANEW

SULENS

NONYAC

GLIBEO

Can you please stop chatting with your friends and start shoveling like I asked you to do?

I'm watching educational videos posted by friends.

WT Cha Doing?

Just Chillin Like a Snowman

LOL

SHE TOLD HER SON TO GET OFF FACEBOOK AND TWITTER TO DO HIS CHORES, BUT HE PREFERRED ----

Now arrange the circled letters to form the surprise answer, as suggested by the above cartoon.

Print answer here

JUMBLE®

Unscramble these six Jumbles, one letter
to each square, to form six ordinary words.

RAWDOT

HETMIR

GURYNH

SURCUK

GARFOE

LARPUL

It's nice of you to
cheer them on.

Let's go, Dad!

C'mon, guys!
Dig in!
You can do it!

EVEN THOUGH HE COULDN'T
PARTICIPATE WITH HIS TEAM
AT THE TUG OF WAR,
HE WAS ----

Now arrange the circled letters to form
the surprise answer, as suggested by the
above cartoon.

Print answer here

JUMBLE®

Unscramble these six Jumbles, one letter to each square, to form six ordinary words.

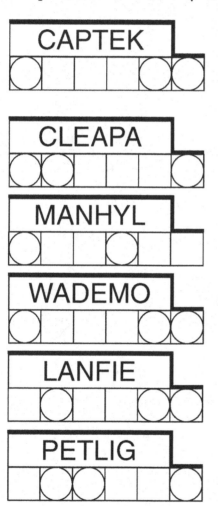

CAPTEK

CLEAPA

MANHYL

WADEMO

LANFIE

PETLIG

Hey! Pipe down.

Let's go, Yankees!!!

I'm a die-hard Red Sox fan!

I've been a Yankees fan my whole life!

| YANKEES | 0 | 2 | 0 | 0 | | | |
| RED SOX | 1 | 0 | 1 | 0 | | | |

THE STANDS AT THE BASEBALL GAME WERE ---

Now arrange the circled letters to form the surprise answer, as suggested by the above cartoon.

Print answer here

" ◯◯◯◯◯◯◯ " ◯◯◯◯   ◯◯◯◯◯◯

JUMBLE®

Unscramble these six Jumbles, one letter to each square, to form six ordinary words.

EESMAS

TRUVIE

CILAPD

DARIOH

NOUEND

KEANSH

We have all these orders. I don't know what to do.

I've got this. I've handled much worse in the Army. Hand me the cajun spices.

WHEN THE RETIRED ARMY COOK BECAME A CHEF, HE WAS ALREADY A ----

Now arrange the circled letters to form the surprise answer, as suggested by the above cartoon.

Print answer here

JUMBLE®

Unscramble these six Jumbles, one letter
to each square, to form six ordinary words.

WEAKAN

TVRREE

BIYLUS

GIDOIN

SULHEB

RELHAB

I never dreamed the view would be so beautiful, especially with you here.

Wow! You're taking my breath away.

HE MET THE WOMAN OF HIS
DREAMS ON THE BALLOON
RIDE BECAUSE ---

Now arrange the circled letters to form
the surprise answer, as suggested by the
above cartoon.

Print answer here

JUMBLE®

Unscramble these six Jumbles, one letter to each square, to form six ordinary words.

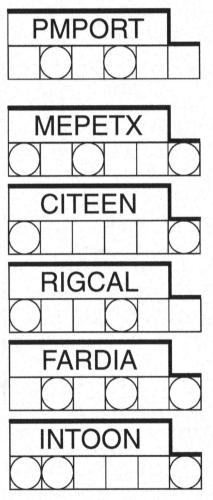

PMPORT

MEPETX

CITEEN

RIGCAL

FARDIA

INTOON

WORKING WITH PLUTONIUM IS SO TRICKY BECAUSE OF THE ---

Now arrange the circled letters to form the surprise answer, as suggested by the above cartoon.

Print answer here

JUMBLE®

Unscramble these six Jumbles, one letter to each square, to form six ordinary words.

RIEGUF

CHERNW

TEAQUE

REYFEL

CADICI

WORDAN

I'm so proud that you're taking this so seriously.

I'm changing everything. Better diet, exercising every day and sticking with it this time.

HE JOINED A GYM AND STARTED EATING BETTER BECAUSE HE WANTED A ----

Now arrange the circled letters to form the surprise answer, as suggested by the above cartoon.

Print answer here

JUMBLE®

Unscramble these six Jumbles, one letter to each square, to form six ordinary words.

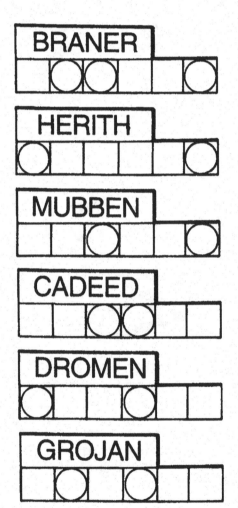

BRANER

HERITH

MUBBEN

CADEED

DROMEN

GROJAN

You're the boss!

WHAT THE TREE SURGEON BECAME.

Now arrange the circled letters to form the surprise answer, as suggested by the above cartoon.

Print answer here

"☐☐☐☐☐☐" ☐☐☐☐☐☐☐

176

JUMBLE®

Unscramble these six Jumbles, one letter to each square, to form six ordinary words.

VOYROG

ROFREV

NABRET

LOVEEV

IPOUTA

RODFIB

Even though you finished last, you still get a medal.

I don't think I can even make it to my car.

MARATHON FINISH

AFTER ATTEMPTING HER FIRST MARATHON, THE RUNNER EXPERIENCED THE ---

Now arrange the circled letters to form the surprise answer, as suggested by the above cartoon.

Print answer here

◯◯◯◯◯ ◯◯ " ◯◯ - ◯◯◯◯ "

JUMBLE®

Unscramble these six Jumbles, one letter to each square, to form six ordinary words.

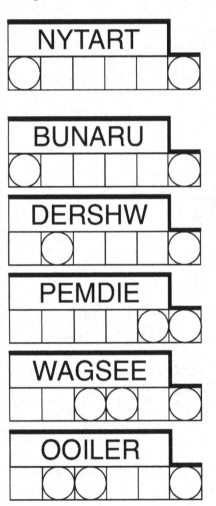

NYTART

BUNARU

DERSHW

PEMDIE

WAGSEE

OOILER

I knew we needed a bigger boat.

Why aren't we moving?

The engine seized up.

THE ZOMBIES' BOAT WAS ---

Now arrange the circled letters to form the surprise answer, as suggested by the above cartoon.

Print answer here

JUMBLE®

Unscramble these six Jumbles, one letter
to each square, to form six ordinary words.

TEBRIT

BUMHAS

NEBING

ROMELA

SEBDIE

BACTOL

Why is the sky blue? Do worms drown? How many kernels does an ear of corn have? Why aren't crows scared of me? Where are you from?

Wow! You sure do have a bunch of questions.

EVEN THOUGH HE DIDN'T
HAVE A BRAIN, THE
SCARECROW HAD ----

Now arrange the circled letters to form
the surprise answer, as suggested by the
above cartoon.

Print answer here

JUMBLE®

Unscramble these six Jumbles, one letter to each square, to form six ordinary words.

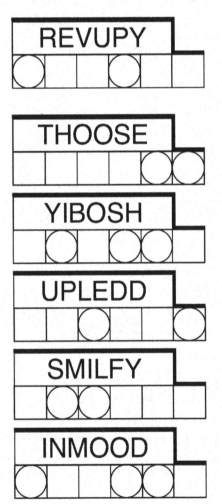

REVUPY

THOOSE

YIBOSH

UPLEDD

SMILFY

INMOOD

How many times does 50 go into 735? You, in the back.

$735 \div 50$

HE WORE HIS GLASSES TO CLASS BECAUSE IT ---

Now arrange the circled letters to form the surprise answer, as suggested by the above cartoon.

Print answer here

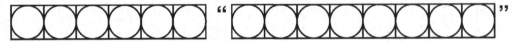

⟨ "   " ⟩

180

JUMBLE®

Unscramble these six Jumbles, one letter to each square, to form six ordinary words.

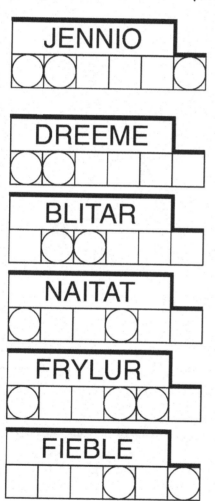

JENNIO

DREEME

BLITAR

NAITAT

FRYLUR

FIEBLE

Hey! That's not how it goes.

WHEN THE SINGER SKIPPED THE CHORUS, IT WAS A ---

Now arrange the circled letters to form the surprise answer, as suggested by the above cartoon.

Print answer here

JUMBLE®

Unscramble these six Jumbles, one letter
to each square, to form six ordinary words.

DIELEY

SLIMAD

HALNIE

TARREY

TERRAH

INIBIK

I'm finally finished.

DRAW ME

WHEN THE ARTIST
COMPLETED HIS WORK,
THE CANVAS WAS ---

Now arrange the circled letters to form
the surprise answer, as suggested by the
above cartoon.

Print answer here

JUMBLE®

Unscramble these six Jumbles, one letter to each square, to form six ordinary words.

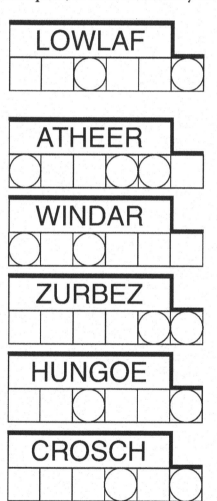

LOWLAF

ATHEER

WINDAR

ZURBEZ

HUNGOE

CROSCH

I'm not paying you to surf the Web

One second, I'm updating my status

THE LAZY REPORTER DIDN'T THINK DEADLINES WERE ---

Now arrange the circled letters to form the surprise answer, as suggested by the above cartoon.

Print answer here

Answers

1. **Jumbles:** ADMIT VAGUE ENABLE BUSHEL
   Answer: Why the miser stopped his clock—TO SAVE TIME

2. **Jumbles:** FRUIT ENTRY DELUXE MODIFY
   Answer: What she said when she saw a mink—
   "I KNOW WHAT YOU'RE FUR"

3. **Jumbles:** GAUZE IMPEL CARPET DENOTE
   Answer: This could be elegant—NEAT LEG

4. **Jumbles:** VILLA SNORT EITHER BOUNCE
   Answer: Something new in neckwear—"NOVEL-TIES"

5. **Jumbles:** GROOM HITCH FRIGID RATIFY
   Answer: She doesn't like to receive one or look one—
   A FRIGHT

6. **Jumbles:** GLEAM HONOR BODILY INWARD
   Answer: Might be a good investment for those who don't
   get everything—A HEARING AID

7. **Jumbles:** BRAND FROZE SOLACE AIRWAY
   Answer: One USED to be this in or at when he enlisted—
   SWORN

8. **Jumbles:** BERTH NIPPY MAINLY COLUMN
   Answer: MEN IN PORT are conspicuous—"PROMINENT"

9. **Jumbles:** WHINE CRACK SUNDAE HEARSE
   Answer: How to cut up in a cab—USE A HACKSAW

10. **Jumbles:** COUGH HENNA FROLIC BYGONE
    Answer: "Again in France?"—"ENCORE"

11. **Jumbles:** LEECH BLOOM GENTLE EMBALM
    Answer: Sounds like a bit of a nut in the army—
    COLONEL ("kernel")

12. **Jumbles:** PATCH SWISH MAGPIE JIGGER
    Answer: Several in a flight—STEPS

13. **Jumbles:** COCOA HASTY PONDER TACKLE
    Answer: This drink might put an end to rumors—SCOTCH

14. **Jumbles:** FAIRY COLON BUNION TEMPER
    Answer: For people down there THIS place could be NO
    FINER—"INFERNO"

15. **Jumbles:** DUCAL FIFTY MENACE IODINE
    Answer: Not to be played with when loaded—DICE

16. **Jumbles:** LEAKY POISE CHALET PHYSIC
    Answer: Far from alert but outwardly sly—"SL-EEP-Y"

17. **Jumbles:** POKER BASIC UNCURL CORPSE
    Answer: A kind of European curtain material—IRON

18. **Jumbles:** TOKEN HUSKY GIBBET FORGET
    Answer: When dropped are meant to be taken up by
    someone else—HINTS

19. **Jumbles:** WEDGE TOXIC COMPEL WEAPON
    Answer: Dragged away—to get married—"TO-WED"

20. **Jumbles:** ROBIN TULIP SHADOW VOYAGE
    Answer: You wouldn't expect to find her at home!—
    A VISITOR

21. **Jumbles:** NEEDY USURP EMERGE INVOKE
    Answer: Where an astronomer might find poetry—
    IN THE "UNI-VERSE"

22. **Jumbles:** GLADE ELEGY MYRIAD ABRUPT
    Answer: What you'll find in the room of your dreams—A BED

23. **Jumbles:** STEED GAILY AMBUSH CALMLY
    Answer: Might be barred in some parks—CAGES

24. **Jumbles:** BOUGH FLUTE WEAKEN DARING
    Answer: You might be powerless to accept this—A TOW

25. **Jumbles:** PIETY AUDIT HAMMER MALTED
    Answer: It's always done in the evening!—THE DAY

26. **Jumbles:** GLOVE PUTTY MILDEW BROGUE
    Answer: How to sell an electric gadget—PLUG IT

27. **Jumbles:** RAINY LATHE CLEAVE FEUDAL
    Answer: Working he gets all THE DIRTIER—THE CLEANER

28. **Jumbles:** ENACT DECAY BECAME PATTER
    Answer: Taken down inside—EATEN

29. **Jumbles:** PARCH SKUNK FACILE NEARLY
    Answer: What the Portuguese neighbor is—SPAIN

30. **Jumbles:** BASIN EXACT ABUSED CANDID
    Answer: Made a dent in the history of literature—DANTE

31. **Jumbles:** GIANT DOILY BOILED KNOTTY
    Answer: What the billy goat said to his mate—
    YOU'RE KIDDING!

32. **Jumbles:** OFTEN SUITE FRUGAL THEORY
    Answer: A loud cry that's quiet to start with—"SH-OUT"

33. **Jumbles:** WHOOP ENSUE DEBATE NUMBER
    Answer: How they knew he was the proprietor—
    HE OWNED UP

34. **Jumbles:** CRUSH DITTO BELONG TINKLE
    Answer: What you might feel like doing after dinner—
    BURSTING

35. **Jumbles:** OBESE PIECE TRIPLE FALLEN
    Answer: An edible part of poppies that many become
    addicted to—"PIES"

36. **Jumbles:** EAGLE THYME HOOKED SHANTY
    Answer: What "a man of leisure" might look down at—
    THE HEELS

37. **Jumbles:** BASIS EXERT CLERGY LAUNCH
    Answer: Checks on a horse!—REINS

38. **Jumbles:** TRYST SINGE BLOUSE MATURE
    Answer: One who won't stand for being painted—A SITTER

39. **Jumbles:** TONIC BISON DONKEY YELLOW
    Answer: Loot taken from a shoe store—"BOOT-Y"

40. **Jumbles:** HAZEL GLORY COUSIN AFRAID
    Answer: What the general said when they ran out of money
    to fight the war—CHARGE!

41. **Jumbles:** RURAL ADMIT ENSIGN BOUGHT
    Answer: What he said all that astrology bull was—"TAURUS"

42. **Jumbles:** BUILT GLOAT DENOTE PANTRY
    Answer: What the ceramics worker was developing—A POT

43. **Jumbles:** RODEO ZOMBI PERSON THWART
    Answer: A traveler has absolutely no chance of getting on
    this line!—THE HORIZON

44. **Jumbles:** EXPEL AWFUL STYMIE LATEST
    Answer: The runner satisfied his thirst after this—
    A FEW LAPS

45. **Jumbles:** ELDER PRIME GIBLET OBLIGE
    Answer: You wouldn't eat it when in this—"(IN)EDIBLE"

46. **Jumbles:** MAIZE WRATH DROWSY SPONGE
    Answer: Why she always had something on whenever he
    asked for a date—SHE WAS MODEST

47. **Jumbles:** LOGIC KNEEL INVENT MYSTIC
    Answer: This light touch could produce laughter in the
    theater—
    A TICKLE

48. **Jumbles:** PAPER CABLE FRENZY HAIRDO
    Answer: Followed in the kitchen—A RECIPE

49. **Jumbles:** ASSAY JOKER ORATOR QUAINT
    Answer: The remainder doesn't work—"REST"

50. **Jumbles:** TRACT SOUSE ADJOIN LAVISH
    Answer: Not the sort of case he expected to find in the
    bungalow—A STAIRCASE

51. **Jumbles:** HENCE YIELD PUTRID MYSELF
Answer: What the millionaire left—MUCH TO BE DESIRED

52. **Jumbles:** SCOUT TANGY NOZZLE GLOOMY
Answer: What a conversation between husband and wife sometimes is—A MONOLOGUE

53. **Jumbles:** MUSTY SIEGE DRIVEL POSTAL
Answer: What tears are—"GLUM" DROPS

54. **Jumbles:** MERGE RANCH EFFACE GAMBIT
Answer: How some prominent family trees were started—BY "GRAFTING"

55. **Jumbles:** FAINT DICED INFIRM JESTER
Answer: What a sponger needs in order to keep afloat—A RAFT OF FRIENDS

56. **Jumbles:** DECRY CHANT GYRATE LAVISH
Answer: How the big vote turned out at the opticians' convention—THE "EYES" HAD IT

57. **Jumbles:** PRIME BELLE PREFIX FORMAT
Answer: The only thing he had against the younger generation was that he was not this—A MEMBER OF IT

58. **Jumbles:** AORTA BANDY PESTLE NEEDLE
Answer: How the students felt about the examination—THEY "DE-TEST-ED" IT

59. **Jumbles:** ASSAY PARTY GUNNER INLAID
Answer: What he quit doing in trying times—TRYING

60. **Jumbles:** BOOTY FORAY METRIC IMPEND
Answer: What some musical performances sound like someone's having—AN "OPERA-TION"

61. **Jumbles:** LILAC JADED PIRATE INVERT
Answer: He felt the only way to multiply happiness was this—TO DIVIDE IT

62. **Jumbles:** RAPID SKIMP RAMROD KENNEL
Answer: What he suffered from when the relatives arrived—"KIN-DREAD"

63. **Jumbles:** HASTY ABASH MARTYR CAMPUS
Answer: What any good junkman knows how to convert—TRASH INTO CASH

64. **Jumbles:** LINGO SORRY INDUCT BUNKER
Answer: He was so healthy it was this—"SICKENING"

65. **Jumbles:** BLANK KNEEL UNFOLD FORGOT
Answer: Beginning horseback riders often do it this way—ON AND OFF

66. **Jumbles:** POWER KAPOK GUILTY LIQUOR
Answer: Some girls close their eyes while kissing, but others do this—LOOK BEFORE THEY "LIP"

67. **Jumbles:** BEGOT ORBIT FINISH PLOWED
Answer: That after-dinner speaker always knew when to rise to the occasion—but seldom this—WHEN TO SIT DOWN

68. **Jumbles:** JETTY NOOSE TURKEY RECTOR
Answer: What he got when he bought that stock—STUCK

69. **Jumbles:** TITLE AWARD YEARLY FERVID
Answer: A confirmed night owl is a man who stays up all night—DAY AFTER DAY

70. **Jumbles:** TOXIN BLOOM REVERE LAUNCH
Answer: It's sometimes a crime to catch fish here, but more often this—A MIRACLE

71. **Jumbles:** OBESE NOVEL JAUNTY DISMAL
Answer: What his wife had a steady job trying to keep him at—A STEADY JOB

72. **Jumbles:** RUSTY SWASH AVENUE LEDGER
Answer: A political platform is something a candidate needs when he hasn't this—A LEG TO STAND ON

73. **Jumbles:** MOSSY QUEUE MATURE EXODUS
Answer: An impatient driver who has to stop for a traffic light usually does this—"SEES RED"

74. **Jumbles:** DOWNY HAVOC CANDID OBLIGE
Answer: What scandal has to be—BAD TO BE GOOD

75. **Jumbles:** ROBOT TULIP CELERY TOTTER
Answer: The best way to better your lot is to do this—A LOT BETTER

76. **Jumbles:** FANCY REARM BODILY GEYSER
Answer: How someone who sowed too many wild oats when he was young might end up looking—"SEEDY"

77. **Jumbles:** WELSH QUAIL YELLOW CAVORT
Answer: What sort of conversation was going on at the library?—A VERY "LOW" ONE

78. **Jumbles:** HIKER VIXEN BUTTON QUARTZ
Answer: Another name for that much talked about baby boom—THE "BIRTHQUAKE"

79. **Jumbles:** RIGOR HAVEN INJURY STURDY
Answer: A handy device for finding furniture in the dark—YOUR SHIN

80. **Jumbles:** TRACT LLAMA SCENIC TRUSTY
Answer: What those old sailing vessels must have provided—MAST TRANSIT

81. **Jumbles:** CHAMP ROUSE HITHER FUMBLE
Answer: Snacks meant to refresh often end up doing this—"REFLESH"

82. **Jumbles:** ESSAY BRINY EMBARK COUPLE
Answer: What a person who believes in fortune-tellers might be—A "SEER" SUCKER

83. **Jumbles:** CHAIR MEALY RATIFY EXPEND
Answer: What a stuffed shirt often goes with—AN EMPTY HEAD

84. **Jumbles:** FRIAR TESTY ENTIRE HELMET
Answer: Sometimes a police dog is the only law with this—TEETH IN IT

85. **Jumbles:** CHOKE TRULY PALACE TERROR
Answer: It could be the best investment on earth!—EARTH

86. **Jumbles:** BATON PIANO STICKY CAUGHT
Answer: When dentists aren't, their patients are—PAINSTAKING

87. **Jumbles:** BERYL APPLY FILLET MORBID
Answer: The best wine after a long voyage—PORT

88. **Jumbles:** INLET HAIRY INFUSE PRYING
Answer: The pianist was a musician to this—HIS FINGERTIPS

89. **Jumbles:** VOUCH FAUNA CONVEX APPEAR
Answer: A prejudiced guy is down on anything he's not this—UP ON

90. **Jumbles:** AMUSE OPERA JARGON PARDON
Answer: What the tuba player's kids called him—"OOM-PA-PA"

91. **Jumbles:** FAIRY BARON GYRATE NUANCE
Answer: What the flag company had—A BANNER YEAR

92. **Jumbles:** MUSTY TWILL JUGGLE SALUTE
Answer: What the feuding brothers faced in the inheritance dispute—A TEST OF WILLS

93. **Jumbles:** JUDGE BEFIT GAMBIT INFORM
Answer: How the body builder felt after a haircut—FIT AND TRIMMED

94. **Jumbles:** ARMOR LEAKY DAWNED VALISE
Answer: What drivers called the slippery road—SKID ROW

95. **Jumbles:** SPURN FLAME BOTTLE PONDER
Answer: What happened to the balding actor?—HE LOST HIS PART

96. **Jumbles:** SCARF UNITY FLORAL PATTER
Answer: What the guest of honor received at his testimonial dinner—A ROAST

97. **Jumbles:** SHEAF SCOUR BLOUSE TREMOR
Answer: Where home remodelers learn their trade—
AT "RE-FORM" SCHOOL

98. **Jumbles:** STUNG VAGUE CROUCH JAGUAR
Answer: What the switchboard operator was at the end of
the day—RUNG OUT

99. **Jumbles:** BROIL NOBLE AUTHOR LOTION
Answer: When the pilot's son arrived he was—HEIR-BORN

100. **Jumbles:** HAVOC ELDER ARTERY HUMBLE
Answer: The kind of life some snakes lead—CHARMED

101. **Jumbles:** BISON GUISE SIMILE SIPHON
Answer: What the donut baker gave his son when he
retired—THE HOLE BUSINESS

102. **Jumbles:** GROOM COUPE FUTILE MOTION
Answer: Where children sometimes try to send their
parents—ON A GUILT TRIP

103. **Jumbles:** BULLY FLOUR ZEALOT MURMUR
Answer: What the tennis player said when he lost the
game—"MY FAULT"

104. **Jumbles:** HOUSE FETID CATNIP CHOSEN
Answer: The cameraman met his newspaper deadline with
this—A PHOTO FINISH

105. **Jumbles:** TRIPE MILKY NICETY PIGEON
Answer: What the monarch used on the newborn heir—
A KING PIN

106. **Jumbles:** STOOP LATCH CASHEW TURNIP
Answer: Always sought but never bought—HAPPINESS

107. **Jumbles:** TARDY IVORY ANKLET TIMELY
Answer: What some leave behind when getting away from it
all—VERY LITTLE

108. **Jumbles:** AIDED FORUM CEMENT FELLOW
Answer: What the fire inspector discovered—AN OLD FLAME

109. **Jumbles:** DELVE BORAX EMBRYO SLEEPY
Answer: What the weightlifter found at his favorite
hangout—BAR BELLES

110. **Jumbles:** EMERY BRAND CLERGY FINALE
Answer: Something he got when he joined the knitting
class—THE NEEDLE

111. **Jumbles:** TITHE GOOEY UNSEEN MARTYR
Answer: The horse with the overly negative attitude was a
—"NEIGH-SAYER"

112. **Jumbles:** ALBUM AGONY MUTATE VOYAGE
Answer: Even though it was cold and dry outside, inside the
coffee shop it was—MUGGY

113. **Jumbles:** CHESS ALLOW VIOLET WALNUT
Answer: After attempting to win for years, he finished first—
AT LAST

114. **Jumbles:** SWIFT DODGE SOCIAL PAROLE
Answer: All the other ghosts enjoyed being with Casper
because he was always in—GOOD SPIRITS

115. **Jumbles:** PRAWN WEIGH SOCKET GUITAR
Answer: The popularity of the restaurant resulted in
customers becoming—WAITERS

116. **Jumbles:** RHYME ROBOT SPEEDY BANISH
Answer: Their hike in Alaska was going along just fine until
they ran into a—"BEAR-IER"

117. **Jumbles:** MUSIC ADAGE BARREL GUTTER
Answer: She woke up late, but she wasn't this—ALARMED

118. **Jumbles:** GUMBO MINUS PRETTY BEHIND
Answer: After years without striking, the picketers had a—
RE-UNION

119. **Jumbles:** ARENA GRAND METRIC BEATEN
Answer: The butchers' convention featured a—
"MEAT" AND GREET

120. **Jumbles:** RIVER ONION TURKEY AWHILE
Answer: Construction on the new gym wasn't going well,
but everything would—WORK OUT

121. **Jumbles:** YOUNG WIPER SHROUD ABRUPT
Answer: If the archeologist's assistant didn't improve, he'd—
BE HISTORY

122. **Jumbles:** SPURN SKIMP PUBLIC HYPHEN
Answer: When she realized how long it would take to
remove all the corn husks, she said—SHUCKS

123. **Jumbles:** GUEST STYLE GUITAR MOTION
Answer: Big Bird wasn't worried about retirement because
he had a—NEST EGG

124. **Jumbles:** BRING BISON COLUMN LUXURY
Answer: After the heat went out in the school, the math
class featured—"NUMB-BURRS"

125. **Jumbles:** FOAMY BEACH SIDING BOTTLE
Answer: He was stranded at sea, and his buddy was—
IN THE SAME BOAT

126. **Jumbles:** USURP ALIAS MATTER CANYON
Answer: Levi Strauss' success selling denim jeans was a
result of him being a—SMARTY-PANTS

127. **Jumbles:** ADMIT THUMP COERCE IMPORT
Answer: When he didn't buy his wife the diamond ring she
was hoping for, he—PAID THE PRICE

128. **Jumbles:** OPERA GUPPY DEFUSE FORAGE
Answer: Their view of the Grand Canyon was—
"GORGE-OUS"

129. **Jumbles:** TWINE SWEPT TROPHY DEARLY
Answer: The pioneer got so excited after seeing the
homestead that his wife said—SETTLE DOWN

130. **Jumbles:** MADLY MOUND CASINO PUPPET
Answer: To honor WWII's heroes, architect Friedrich St.
Florian came up with an idea that was—MONUMENTAL

131. **Jumbles:** OMEGA APART PROVEN COUSIN
Answer: The politician had never slept in a tent and didn't
like the—"CAMP-PAIN"

132. **Jumbles:** COVET TOXIN SPRAWL DEVOUR
Answer: She couldn't eat her prize tomato because it had
been—SPOILED ROTTEN

133. **Jumbles:** HONOR COCOA HOBNOB GLOOMY
Answer: When the owl realized he was a ghost, he said—
BOO-HOO

134. **Jumbles:** STOMP WEDGE HANGAR UPROOT
Answer: Lassie bought the house because the
neighborhood had—GONE TO THE DOGS

135. **Jumbles:** OCCUR HARSH BEMOAN SKETCH
Answer: There was no charge for the shingles because they
were—ON THE HOUSE

136. **Jumbles:** UNITY VIDEO ELICIT FISCAL
Answer: They got the painting appraised because they—
VALUED IT

137. **Jumbles:** ABOVE TWANG INLAND TRAUMA
Answer: The handsome bounty hunter was a—
WANTED MAN

138. **Jumbles:** WEAVE TOTAL SCORCH SUNKEN
Answer: The detective thought he'd be handling the
investigation, but that—WASN'T THE CASE

139. **Jumbles:** ARENA HITCH BOTTOM GRAVEL
Answer: The play would be a disaster if the actors didn't get
their—ACT TOGETHER

140. **Jumbles:** DODGE BRAVE AROUND INTACT
Answer: The rock group was so bad that the audience left.
They were—"A-BAND-ONED"

141. **Jumbles:** SHYLY GUEST VISUAL OFFEND
Answer: When he blew all his money playing slot machines, poker, etc., he was in—"LOSS" VEGAS

142. **Jumbles:** GROOM SWOON MODEST BICKER
Answer: The TV chef came up with the new salad concept in her—DRESSING ROOM

143. **Jumbles:** CLOAK DRINK REMOVE SKIMPY
Answer: Before signing the contract for the stone home, he wanted to make sure it was—ROCK-SOLID

144. **Jumbles:** RELIC STYLE USEFUL TOWARD
Answer: The doctor was puzzled by the woman's illness. He'd find a remedy, he was very—"CURE-IOUS"

145. **Jumbles:** WEIGH MOOSE VIABLE UNRULY
Answer: The fireplace in their new home made for a nice—HOUSEWARMING

146. **Jumbles:** PRUNE MERGE STINKY MATTER
Answer: At Santa's workshop, there was plenty of—MERRYMAKING

147. **Jumbles:** WATCH ROUND MENACE UPDATE
Answer: After spitting out his bubble gum on the sidewalk, the teen was—CHEWED OUT

148. **Jumbles:** WHILE QUACK JOCKEY AFLOAT
Answer: The math teacher liked teaching addition and subtraction—EQUALLY

149. **Jumbles:** DITCH GOUGE FOSSIL GAGGLE
Answer: Asked if there'd be morning mist, the weatherman didn't have the—FOGGIEST IDEA

150. **Jumbles:** EXCEL APART CLINIC KNOTTY
Answer: The doctor would eventually feel at home in the new town, if he had enough—PATIENCE

151. **Jumbles:** EVOKE CHILD GEYSER HONCHO
Answer: When they toasted at the New Year's Eve party, everyone was—IN GOOD "CHEERS"

152. **Jumbles:** GRIME MESSY BITTEN VOYAGE
Answer: After playing tennis all day, he was happy for a meal with—BIG SERVINGS

153. **Jumbles:** DOUGH SOUPY ONWARD UNJUST
Answer: When the producer told him he needed to switch microphones, he said—SOUNDS GOOD

154. **Jumbles:** TEASE RELIC BEHOLD CLAMMY
Answer: The author who wrote from his basement had a—BEST "CELLAR"

155. **Jumbles:** RAZOR HAIRY BELIEF CATTLE
Answer: The cardiologist was able to walk to work because he lived in the—HEART OF THE CITY

156. **Jumbles:** QUAIL ODDLY TAWDRY CHANGE
Answer: Sleepy Hollow's horseman had finished breakfast and was ready to—HEAD OUT

157. **Jumbles:** CARGO NINTH DEPICT EUREKA
Answer: To figure out how to send orange juice to WWII troops, the researchers—CONCENTRATED

158. **Jumbles:** GOOSE HARSH PROVEN CAMPUS
Answer: With so many cappuccino and latte drinkers having bad colds, the café was a—"COUGH-EE" SHOP

159. **Jumbles:** DITCH BRAVO MANAGE GARLIC
Answer: The weasel didn't like his pushy cousin because his cousin liked to—BADGER HIM

160. **Jumbles:** HELLO BIRCH SUFFIX SHROUD
Answer: An electric guitar with just one string is—"CHORDLESS"

161. **Jumbles:** FAMOUS TANGLE REDUCE HERMIT HOMELY TEACUP
Answer: After the wind blew the sombrero off her head, he picked it up for her—AT THE DROP OF A HAT

162. **Jumbles:** MANAGE AFLOAT TRENCH INHALE COBALT UNFAIR
Answer: When Little League baseball was created in 1939, it was popular with players and fans—RIGHT OFF THE BAT

163. **Jumbles:** ZIPPER HARBOR CHANCE KITTEN UNEASY TRENDY
Answer: They jumped out of the plane together and were able to—"CHUTE" THE BREEZE

164. **Jumbles:** SPRING SHREWD AFRAID BUTANE FEWEST EMBARK
Answer: He decided to climb Mount Everest because the world's tallest mountain—"PEAKED" HIS INTEREST

165. **Jumbles:** CASHEW WETTER CAREER SLOWLY UNPACK LAVISH
Answer: When it came to which new windows to buy, the—CHOICE WAS CLEAR

166. **Jumbles:** REVERT LIQUOR AWAKEN UNLESS CANYON OBLIGE
Answer: She told her son to get off Facebook and Twitter, but he preferred—SOCIAL "NOTWORKING"

167. **Jumbles:** TOWARD HERMIT HUNGRY RUCKUS FORAGE PLURAL
Answer: Even though he couldn't participate with his team at the tug of war, he was—PULLING FOR THEM

168. **Jumbles:** PACKET PALACE HYMNAL MEADOW FINALE PIGLET
Answer: The stands at the baseball game were—"TEAMING" WITH PEOPLE

169. **Jumbles:** SESAME VIRTUE PLACID HAIRDO UNDONE SHAKEN
Answer: When the retired army cook became a chef, he was already a—SEASONED VETERAN

170. **Jumbles:** AWAKEN REVERT BUSILY INDIGO BUSHEL HERBAL
Answer: He met the woman of his dreams on the balloon ride because—LOVE WAS IN THE AIR

171. **Jumbles:** PROMPT EXEMPT ENTICE GARLIC AFRAID NOTION
Answer: Working with plutonium is so tricky because of the—ELEMENT OF DANGER

172. **Jumbles:** FIGURE WRENCH EQUATE FREELY ACIDIC ONWARD
Answer: He joined a gym and started eating better because he wanted a—NEW "WEIGH" OF LIFE

173. **Jumbles:** BARREN HITHER BENUMB DECADE MODERN JARGON
Answer: What the tree surgeon became—"BRANCH" MANAGER

174. **Jumbles:** GROOVY FERVOR BANTER EVOLVE UTOPIA FORBID
Answer: After attempting her first marathon, the runner experienced the—AGONY OF "DE-FEET"

175. **Jumbles:** TYRANT AUBURN SHREWD IMPEDE SEWAGE ORIOLE
Answer: The zombies' boat was—DEAD IN THE WATER

176. **Jumbles:** BITTER AMBUSH BENIGN MORALE BESIDE COBALT
Answer: Even though he didn't have a brain, the scarecrow had—A LOT ON HIS MIND

177. **Jumbles:** PURVEY SOOTHE BOYISH PUDDLE FLIMSY DOMINO
Answer: He wore his glasses to class because it—HELPED "DIVISION"

178. **Jumbles:** ENJOIN REDEEM TRIBAL ATTAIN FLURRY BELIEF
Answer: When the singer skipped the chorus, it was a—REFRAIN

179. **Jumbles:** EYELID DISMAL INHALE ARTERY RATHER BIKINI
Answer: When the artist completed his work, the canvas was—BEHIND HIS IDEA

180. **Jumbles:** FALLOW HEATER INWARD BUZZER ENOUGH SCORCH
Answer: The lazy reporter didn't think deadlines were—WORTH HER WHILE

Need More Jumbles?

Jumble® Books

More than 175 puzzles each!

Cowboy Jumble®
ISBN: 978-1-62937-355-3

Jammin' Jumble®
ISBN: 1-57243-844-4

Java Jumble®
ISBN: 978-1-60078-415-6

Jazzy Jumble®
ISBN: 978-1-57243-962-7

Jet Set Jumble®
ISBN: 978-1-60078-353-1

Joyful Jumble®
ISBN: 978-1-60078-079-0

Juke Joint Jumble®
ISBN: 978-1-60078-295-4

Jumble® Anniversary
ISBN: 987-1-62937-734-6

Jumble® at Work
ISBN: 1-57243-147-4

Jumble® Ballet
ISBN: 978-1-62937-616-5

Jumble® Birthday
ISBN: 978-1-62937-652-3

Jumble® Celebration
ISBN: 978-1-60078-134-6

Jumble® Circus
ISBN: 978-1-60078-739-3

Jumble® Cuisine
ISBN: 978-1-62937-735-3

Jumble® Drag Race
ISBN: 978-1-62937-483-3

Jumble® Ever After
ISBN: 978-1-62937-785-8

Jumble® Explorer
ISBN: 978-1-60078-854-3

Jumble® Explosion
ISBN: 978-1-60078-078-3

Jumble® Fever
ISBN: 1-57243-593-3

Jumble® Fiesta
ISBN: 1-57243-626-3

Jumble® Fun
ISBN: 1-57243-379-5

Jumble® Galaxy
ISBN: 978-1-60078-583-2

Jumble® Garden
ISBN: 978-1-62937-653-0

Jumble® Genius
ISBN: 1-57243-896-7

Jumble® Geography
ISBN: 978-1-62937-615-8

Jumble® Getaway
ISBN: 978-1-60078-547-4

Jumble® Gold
ISBN: 978-1-62937-354-6

Jumble® Grab Bag
ISBN: 1-57243-273-X

Jumble® Gymnastics
ISBN: 978-1-62937-306-5

Jumble® Jackpot
ISBN: 1-57243-897-5

Jumble® Jailbreak
ISBN: 978-1-62937-002-6

Jumble® Jambalaya
ISBN: 978-1-60078-294-7

Jumble® Jamboree
ISBN: 1-57243-696-4

Jumble® Jitterbug
ISBN: 978-1-60078-584-9

Jumble® Journey
ISBN: 978-1-62937-549-6

Jumble® Jubilation
ISBN: 978-1-62937-784-1

Jumble® Jubilee
ISBN: 1-57243-231-4

Jumble® Juggernaut
ISBN: 978-1-60078-026-4

Jumble® Junction
ISBN: 1-57243-380-9

Jumble® Jungle
ISBN: 978-1-57243-961-0

Jumble® Kingdom
ISBN: 978-1-62937-079-8

Jumble® Knockout
ISBN: 978-1-62937-078-1

Jumble® Madness
ISBN: 1-892049-24-4

Jumble® Magic
ISBN: 978-1-60078-795-9

Jumble® Marathon
ISBN: 978-1-60078-944-1

Jumble® Neighbor
ISBN: 978-1-62937-845-9

Jumble® Parachute
ISBN: 978-1-62937-548-9

Jumble® Safari
ISBN: 978-1-60078-675-4

Jumble® See & Search
ISBN: 1-57243-549-6

Jumble® See & Search 2
ISBN: 1-57243-734-0

Jumble® Sensation
ISBN: 978-1-60078-548-1

Jumble® Surprise
ISBN: 1-57243-320-5

Jumble® Symphony
ISBN: 978-1-62937-131-3

Jumble® Theater
ISBN: 978-1-62937-484-03

Jumble® University
ISBN: 978-1-62937-001-9

Jumble® Unleashed
ISBN: 978-1-62937-844-2

Jumble® Vacation
ISBN: 978-1-60078-796-6

Jumble® Wedding
ISBN: 978-1-62937-307-2

Jumble® Workout
ISBN: 978-1-60078-943-4

Jumpin' Jumble®
ISBN: 978-1-60078-027-1

Lunar Jumble®
ISBN: 978-1-60078-853-6

Monster Jumble®
ISBN: 978-1-62937-213-6

Mystic Jumble®
ISBN: 978-1-62937-130-6

Outer Space Jumble®
ISBN: 978-1-60078-416-3

Rainy Day Jumble®
ISBN: 978-1-60078-352-4

Ready, Set, Jumble®
ISBN: 978-1-60078-133-0

Rock 'n' Roll Jumble®
ISBN: 978-1-60078-674-7

Royal Jumble®
ISBN: 978-1-60078-738-6

Sports Jumble®
ISBN: 1-57243-113-X

Summer Fun Jumble®
ISBN: 1-57243-114-8

Touchdown Jumble®
ISBN: 978-1-62937-212-9

Travel Jumble®
ISBN: 1-57243-198-9

TV Jumble®
ISBN: 1-57243-461-9

Oversize Jumble® Books

More than 500 puzzles each!

Generous Jumble®
ISBN: 1-57243-385-X

Giant Jumble®
ISBN: 1-57243-349-3

Gigantic Jumble®
ISBN: 1-57243-426-0

Jumbo Jumble®
ISBN: 1-57243-314-0

The Very Best of Jumble® BrainBusters
ISBN: 1-57243-845-2

Jumble® Crosswords™

More than 175 puzzles each!

More Jumble® Crosswords™
ISBN: 1-57243-386-8

Jumble® Crosswords™ Jackpot
ISBN: 1-57243-615-8

Jumble® Crosswords™ Jamboree
ISBN: 1-57243-787-1

Jumble® BrainBusters™

More than 175 puzzles each!

Jumble® BrainBusters™
ISBN: 1-892049-28-7

Jumble® BrainBusters™ II
ISBN: 1-57243-424-4

Jumble® BrainBusters™ III
ISBN: 1-57243-463-5

Jumble® BrainBusters™ IV
ISBN: 1-57243-489-9

Jumble® BrainBusters™ 5
ISBN: 1-57243-548-8

Jumble® BrainBusters™ Bonanza
ISBN: 1-57243-616-6

Boggle™ BrainBusters™
ISBN: 1-57243-592-5

Boggle™ BrainBusters™ 2
ISBN: 1-57243-788-X

Jumble® BrainBusters™ Junior
ISBN: 1-892049-29-5

Jumble® BrainBusters™ Junior II
ISBN: 1-57243-425-2

Fun in the Sun with Jumble® BrainBusters™
ISBN: 1-57243-733-2